Other Scribner Library Books by ALFRED MORGAN

THE FIRST BOOK OF RADIO AND ELECTRONICS

FIRST CHEMISTRY BOOK FOR BOYS AND GIRLS

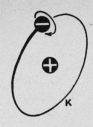

Adventures
in Electrochemistry

by

ALFRED MORGAN

WITH DIAGRAMS BY THE AUTHOR

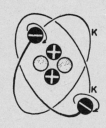

CHARLES SCRIBNER'S SONS *New York*

Library of Congress Cataloging in Publication Data

Morgan, Alfred Powell, 1889-1972
   Adventures in electrochemistry.

   (The Scribner library)

   Includes index.
   SUMMARY: Discusses the historical background and present-day importance of electrochemistry and includes instructions for constructing apparatus and performing experiments.
   1.   Electrochemistry—Juvenile literature.
[1.   Electrochemistry]   I.   Title.
TP256.M6   1977   541'.37   76-54836
ISBN 0-684-14754-8

1 3 5 7 9 11 13 15 17 19 C/P 20 18 16 14 12 10 8 6 4 2

Printed in the United States of America

Contents

Adventures in Electrochemistry

Chapter One

A Definition of Electrochemistry

ITS BEGINNING AND ITS PRESENT-DAY IMPORTANCE

An old maxim states: "You cannot make a silk purse out of a sow's ear." These words stress the fact that suitable materials are always necessary in order to make something. ELECTROCHEMISTRY provides industry with some of its most useful and valuable materials.

If the industrial world were without the materials produced by electrochemical processes, it is probable that most machinery would be heavier, slower, more cumbersome, and shorter-lived. There would be no low-cost aluminum, and little of the PURE copper which is necessary for wires in the electrical industry. They are both electrochemical products. Many things would cost more to manufacture. Some useful metals and alloys * cannot be produced economically except by electrochemical methods.

* A substance composed of two or more metals.

Much electrochemical magic lies hidden from our eyes. For example, we do not see the life-saving chlorine which has been added to the water stored in reservoirs, or the strength-giving metal molybdenum used in automobile axles, etc. We do not always realize that many exceedingly strong alloy steels, fertilizers, abrasives, printing plates, and the light-weight aluminum in cooking utensils, doors, window frames and aircraft are gifts of electrochemistry.

THE DEFINITION OF ELECTROCHEMISTRY

Electrochemistry is that branch of chemistry which uses ELECTRICAL ENERGY to facilitate or carry on the chemical processes and changes called CHEMICAL REACTIONS.

Electrochemical reaction may be accomplished by:
1. electrolytic action
2. electrothermic action, or
3. the discharge of electricity through gases.

Electrolytic action is the chemical process which takes place when an electric current is passed through certain solutions. Electrothermic action is the chemical action which is caused by the high temperatures which an electric current can generate.

Electrochemistry also includes those reactions in which electricity is generated by chemical action.

A Hobby

The science of electrochemistry is interesting and instructive territory for the amateur scientist to explore.

Some amazing experiments in which electricity and chemistry both play a part can be performed on a kitchen table. Incidentally, several of the most fundamental and valuable processes in commercial electrochemistry were discovered by very young men who spent time experimenting in this field.

THE BEGINNING OF ELECTROCHEMISTRY

The history of electrochemistry is romantic; it is filled with tales of disappointment, tragedy, success, and wealth.

Electrochemical processes require electric current. The existence of electric CURRENT and the means for producing it were unknown until the year 1800. That year Alessandro Volta, an Italian scientist, discovered that when two unlike metals are in contact with paper or cloth which has been moistened with a solution of table salt in water, they will produce an electric current. The voltaic pile, as the original form of Volta's astonishing invention was called, was the first electric battery. It was the first source of electrical energy for electrochemical experiments. Electrochemistry was born with Volta's pile. Many discoveries in the field of electrochemistry were made during the early years of the nineteenth century. These discoveries were scientific facts and methods previously unknown to scientists. They were new scientific knowledge. The application of electrochemical processes in industry to produce useful materials had to wait for an era of larger and cheaper quantities of electric current than could be produced by batteries. Commercial electrochemical processes had to wait until powerful electric generators driven by water power were developed. An electrochemist is interested only in electric power which costs a fraction of a dollar per kilowatt hour. A kilowatt hour is the amount of electrical energy used by a 100-watt electric lamp in 10 hours. Higher-priced energy would make the processes too expensive. The commercial uses of electrochemistry are about one hundred years old.

How Does Electrochemistry Utilize Electric Current?

The answer to this question is that the electric current is used to produce a chemical reaction. One method is to convert electrical energy into intense heat in an electric furnace. The heat brings about the desired chemical reaction. The second method, called ELECTROLYSIS, is to cause a chemical reaction to take place by passing an electric current through a solution, or through a bath of molten material. Pure copper, silver, and many of the rare metals are procured through electrolysis.

Ways in which the amateur chemist, equipped with a few dry cells, can employ electricity to break down chemical compounds and build up new ones, are described later in this book. You will probably understand these methods better if you first read how some of the important discoveries in electrochemistry were made.

The First Electrochemical Discovery

There is good evidence that three scientists named Paetz, Van Troostwick, and Deiman discovered, as early as 1790, that the discharge of a Leyden jar was capable of decomposing a small quantity of water. They passed very powerful discharges into water by means of fine gold wires and were able to collect small quantities of the gases which were released. The discharge of a Leyden jar is gone in a fraction of a second, and this demonstration did not have much significance until steady electric current was available.

Sir Humphry Davy is often wrongly credited with discovering that electricity is a chemical agent. The first successful attempt to use an ELECTRIC CURRENT to bring about a chemical reaction was made in 1800 by two English scientists, Sir Anthony Carlisle and William Nicholson. Both men were friends of Sir Joseph Banks, President of the Royal Society of London. Banks received the first announcement of Volta's discovery of a new source of electric current in a private letter from Volta in March, 1800. Before reading Volta's letter to the Royal Society (June, 1800), Banks showed it to Carlisle and Nicholson. These men immediately grasped the immense possibilities of the new force. They were among the first of the pioneers to experiment with the electric current produced by Volta's pile.

During their experiments, hoping to secure better contact between two wires forming part of a circuit which included a voltaic pile, Carlisle and Nicholson connected the ends of the wires with a drop of water. An essential of scientific discovery is observation. Carlisle and Nicholson observed the immediate formation of tiny bubbles in the drop of water and concluded that the gas which formed the bubbles was HYDROGEN. They realized that they had at hand a new implement which chemists might use to pry apart chemical compounds. It might also build up new ones. So they set about producing more hydrogen by purposely sending the current from a voltaic pile through water. Their exuberance knew no bounds when they found that the electric current decomposed the water into TWO gases: HYDROGEN and OXYGEN. Here, before their astonished eyes, electricity had pried molecules apart, had separated molecules of water into their constituent atoms. Nothing like that had ever been known to happen. The news spread like wildfire through the scientific world. A vast new territory in the Land of Science had been opened to exploration.

A Young Man Named Jöns Jakob Berzelius

Much of the history of electrochemistry is a story of the experiments of young men with youthful curiosity, imagination, and patience which unlocked many scientific secrets. At the time that Carlisle and Nicholson were puttering around in their laboratory with voltaic piles and drops of water, there was a twenty-one-year-old orphan named Jöns Jakob Berzelius at the University of Upsala in Sweden. He was there preparing for a degree in medicine. Young Berzelius was an earnest youth, accustomed to hardship. For years he had worked on his stepfather's farm, sleeping in a room which was also the storage bin for the potato crop. He dreamed of being a clergyman or doctor. He decided to quit the farm and go to school in order to realize his ambition. He asked his stepfather for his wages. Four dollars and a pair of woolen stockings were the meager recompense he received from the stingy stepfather for years of drudgery.

At the University young Berzelius supported himself by tutoring others not so quick to learn. He became interested in experimental chemistry. Students were at liberty to work in the laboratory once a week only. That was not often enough for Berzelius. Several times he slipped in while the instructor was away and performed some experiments. Eventually he was caught while in the midst of an experiment of his own devising. He was rebuked but his unusual interest and zeal in chemistry won him the right to use the laboratory in his spare time.

When news of Carlisle and Nicholson's discovery that an electric current would decompose water reached Berzelius, he tried dividing compounds other than water by means of current from a voltaic pile. He soon found that water was not the only compound that could be pried apart by an electric current. He discovered that solutions of metallic salts could be broken up and that metals always went to the positive side of his electro-chemical apparatus and non-metals went to the negative side.

It was not possible for Berzelius or any other scientist of those days to know why this happens. He was unwittingly touching upon one of the most remarkable facts known to modern science—the fact that in every atom and molecule of the substances we call matter there are equal definite quantities of positive and negative electricity. For example, if an atom contains 11 particles of negative electricity (called ELECTRONS), it will also contain 11 particles with a positive charge (called PROTONS). The name Jöns Jakob Berzelius shines in the history of chemical science. In the experiments of this ex-farm boy were the beginnings of the huge science of electrochemistry. Among many notable scientific achievements, Berzelius discovered the element THORIUM and was co-discoverer of the elements CERIUM and SELENIUM. He was first to separate SILICON from its compounds and prove it to be an element and first to isolate and exhibit ZIRCONIUM.

Chapter Two

We Look at Atoms, Elements, and Molecules · *A YOUNG MAN NAMED HUMPHRY DAVY · THE ELECTRIC FURNACE*

Modern scientists have good reason to believe that all matter on earth, in fact, all matter in the universe, is made of tiny particles called ATOMS. Approximately 100 different atoms have been discovered. They are called the CHEMICAL ELEMENTS. The names of many of the elements are familiar to us, for example: HYDROGEN, OXYGEN, CARBON, IRON, COPPER, GOLD, HELIUM, PHOSPHORUS, etc. The names of many others, names such as MASURIUM, XENON, NEODYMIUM, PROTOACTINIUM, YTTERBIUM, LUTECIUM, DYSPROSIUM, etc., are usually known only to chemists.

All atoms are so small as to be beyond human perception. The largest is only .00000001 of an inch in diameter, and many are much smaller. The thinnest film of gold leaf is hundreds of atoms thick.

The more than 250,000 different substances in our world are only varied groupings of the atoms of the elements into MOLECULES. A molecule is the smallest portion of an element or a compound that retains chemical identity with a mass of the same substance. For example, an atom of the silvery, waxlike metallic element called sodium, joined with an atom of the element which is a greenish-yellow gas called chlorine, forms a molecule of salt, the common table salt which a chemist calls sodium chloride. Dividing a molecule of salt would separate it into an atom of sodium and an atom of chlorine, neither of which would have the identity of a molecule of salt. We cannot see a single molecule of salt, but we can see a mass of them in the form of the small crystals which we sprinkle on our food to bring out its flavor.

THE ELECTRICAL NATURE OF THE ATOMS

There is good reason to believe that the atoms of all the elements are made up of tiny particles of negative electricity called ELECTRONS, tiny particles of positive electricity called PROTONS, and neutral particles of the same mass as the proton called NEUTRONS.

As yet there is no satisfactory answer to the question, "What is electricity?" Our knowledge of electricity lies in the things that it does rather than in its exact nature.

We can use diagrams to represent what we think the structure and arrangement of the various atoms to be. A dense center portion of each atom called the nucleus, represented by a shaded area in the center of the dia-

We know what electricity DOES but not what it is.

gram, contains all the protons, or particles of positive electricity.

All atomic nuclei, except those of ordinary hydrogen, contain neutrons. It is thought that a neutron is an electrically neutral particle, that is, an uncharged particle. Neutrons, being uncharged, are not repelled by electrons and protons and are able to penetrate nuclei. They are used for bombarding in nuclear disintegration experiments. The number of electrons and the number of protons in each element are equal, thereby giving a neutral atom. Around the central nucleus, the electrons revolve

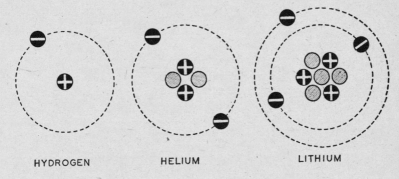

HYDROGEN   HELIUM   LITHIUM

DIAGRAMS OF THE ATOMS OF HYDROGEN, HELIUM, AND LITHIUM

These three elements have the lightest and simplest atoms. The diagrams above are an elementary method of illustrating the structure of an atom. They show the electrons, protons, and neutrons of which atoms are composed. In these diagrams, neutrons are shaded, electrons are indicated by a negative sign, and protons are marked with a positive sign. The protons and neutrons are always at the center, or nucleus, of an atom. The electrons revolve around the nucleus in circular or elliptical paths called SHELLS. Only two electrons can be accommodated in the shell nearest the center, called the "K" shell. The third electron in a lithium atom must revolve in an outer shell called the "L" shell.

MORE REALISTIC

These are more accurate diagrams of the atoms of hydrogen, helium, and lithium than those in the preceding illustration. The shells in which the planetary electrons revolve are not circular flat planes as indicated by the dotted circles. A circle or ellipse traced around a ball like the imaginary line which is the equator of the earth is a true representation of the path of an electron which is revolving in one of the shells of an atom. There are from one to seven shells surrounding the nucleus of an atom, arranged one inside the other like concentric hollow spheres. More than one electron may travel around in the same shell, but each electron has its own special orbit. Each electron also spins on its own axis (indicated by the curved arrows), just as the earth spins on its own axis.

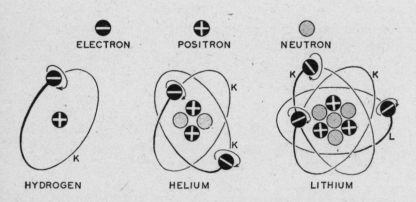

in one or more orbits, or circular or elliptical paths. The best way to indicate the revolving electrons in a diagram of an atom or molecule is to represent them as black dots or balls marked with negative, or minus, signs. The paths they travel are shown as circles or ellipses (called SHELLS). Such a diagram forms a picture somewhat like one of the earth and the planets revolving around the sun. It is not an entirely accurate picture. It does, however, give us a concept of the scientists' mental picture of the atoms.

All atoms of the same element contain the same number and arrangement of protons and electrons. But the atoms of the different elements differ from each other in their component number and arrangement of protons and electrons. There are as many as seven shells surrounding the nucleus of the heavy atoms such as radon, actinium, thorium, protoactinium, and uranium.

An atom of ordinary hydrogen has the simplest structure and is the lightest of all the elements. It has only one planetary, or revolving, electron. Uranium is the heaviest element and has the most complicated atom. Around its heavy nucleus revolve 92 electrons.

Samuel Goudsmit and George Uhlenbeck were both in their early twenties and students at Leiden University, Holland, when they published in 1925 a suggestion which has turned out to be one of the basic discoveries of modern science. They proposed that each planetary electron in an atom, in addition to moving around the positively charged nucleus, spins on its own axis like a top, either clockwise or counterclockwise. This suggestion solved some puzzles which had stood in the way of a more satisfactory understanding of atomic structure and of the infinite universe.

A Young Man Named Humphry Davy

The experiments of young Berzelius, the ex-farm boy, in which he used an electric current to split molecules apart and capture the atoms of which they were composed, were the beginnings of the present-day science of electrochemistry. Berzelius published a scientific paper describing his ingenious work in dividing compounds by means of a voltaic pile, but his discoveries remained largely unnoticed for nearly four years. Four years after publication, a copy of the Berzelius paper fell into the hands of a young English chemist named Humphry Davy. Using Volta's pile and continuing the researches of Berzelius, this young man soon isolated new and strange elements which staggered the imagination of the scientific world. He was the first to isolate and identify the elements POTASSIUM, SODIUM, STRONTIUM, BARIUM, CALCIUM and BORON. These elements were known to exist but only in combination with other elements. They had never been isolated until Davy succeeded in doing so by electrochemical methods.

The name Humphry Davy belonged to one of the most illustrious scientists of all time. Like most other really great men, he had a simple beginning. He was born in the little Cornish town of Penzance near the westernmost tip of England. His parents were poor. While still a lad, Davy was bound as an apothecary's apprentice to a prominent surgeon-apothecary, John Borlase.

This was a stroke of luck for the embryo scientist. Dr. Borlase was a man of much scientific knowledge, and he had a considerable library. He encouraged his apprentice's curiosity and his desire to learn. After the day's work of compounding drugs was finished, young Davy spent his spare time reading, investigating, and experimenting.

Soon after Volta revealed that chemicals could be used to produce an electric current, Davy constructed a voltaic pile and began to experiment with electric current. He found that bright sparks were produced when the two wires connected to the terminals of the pile were rubbed together. Especially brilliant sparks could be produced by attaching charcoal electrodes to the wires. Davy tucked this significant fact away in his mind. He was to make use of it later.

THE FIRST ELECTRIC FURNACE

There was then, and there still is, in London a brilliant association of men of science called the Royal Society, which engages in scientific work and maintains courses of scientific lectures.

At a dignified meeting of this Royal Society in London in the year 1807, we find a slightly undersized young man of fresh complexion and chestnut curls lecturing to the distinguished gathering on some of the chemical reactions caused by an electric current. The high-born and wealthy listeners had paid a large admission fee to hear the young lecturer and to see his demonstrations.

The young man is Humphry Davy, ex-apothecary's apprentice. At this time he is Professor of Chemistry at the Royal Institution. On the lecture table is a small sheet of platinum. On top of the platinum is a block of caustic soda. Caustic soda is the active, sometimes dangerous, substance known in the modern laboratory as SODIUM HYDROXIDE and in the household as lye. Davy's caustic soda block is slightly hollowed on top and the depression is filled with mercury. A wire from a battery dips into the mercury. Another wire leads from the battery to the platinum. The platinum and the mercury are ELECTRODES, or, in other words, the terminals of a source of electric current. An electric current is passing through the caustic soda. Soon the mercury is no longer a mobile fluid; it has become stiff. Davy explains that the stiffened mercury is an amalgam, or alloy, of mercury and sodium. The electric current has produced metallic sodium from sodium hydroxide. In further experiments, he produces some small globules of bright, shiny metallic sodium which are unalloyed with mercury. In still other experiments, the metals barium, strontium, potassium, and magnesium are produced. Electric current in the hands of the right man is proving to be a source of much new scientific knowledge.

Davy's demonstrations aroused great interest in his work. A fund was raised to buy the young savant a larger battery. A few years later, with a battery of 150 cells, Davy showed an astonished audience *an electric light*.

It was his old trick of making sparks with two charcoal electrodes connected to a voltaic pile. Now he was repeating it on a larger scale. Using his powerful battery, he made an electric flame, or "arc," over an inch long sizzle between the charcoal electrodes. Its intense brilliance lighted the whole auditorium. His audience was delighted. A few years later, in 1813, when he wished to experiment with a still more powerful battery, Davy had no difficulty in raising by private subscription the money required to build a battery of 2,000 cells.

The modern electric arc furnace had its beginning in the electric arc discovered by Humphry Davy. Davy

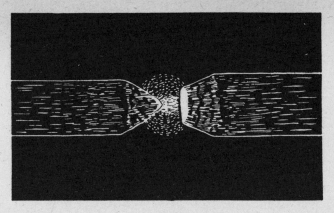

THE ELECTRIC ARC

When two carbon rods, connected to a source of suitable current, are touched together and then drawn apart a short distance, a brilliant, hot electric flame called an arc is formed. From about 1880 to 1915, carbon electrode arcs were used for lighting streets and large interiors. They have been replaced by incandescent and fluorescent lamps. Arcs are still in use but not for illumination. They are now used in electro-chemistry, for welding, for irradiating foods, in military searchlights, in some movie projectors, and in physical therapy. A carbon arc is rich in ultraviolet rays and in light near the violet end of the visible spectrum. Some of the "sun-ray" lamps sold in drugstores are carbon arc lamps. Large, powerful carbon arc lamps are used in many food factories to irradiate foods so that the foods become a source of vitamin D. The high temperature produced in an arc makes it possible to weld steel and iron and other metals with a high melting point.

found the heat of his electric flame to be so intense that it would "melt" everything as readily as the flame of a candle melts wax. In its present form, the electric arc furnace provides the highest temperature available commercially. Temperatures of nearly 7,000 degrees F can be produced. The only limitations in obtaining still higher temperatures in an electric furnace are the materials used for building the furnace. They vanish in smoke long before the highest temperature possible is reached.

ELECTRIC INFERNOS

It is a far cry from Davy's small black sticks of charcoal to modern electric furnace electrodes, which are in some instances carbon rods 15 feet long and 4 feet in diameter. Davy's pencil-sized sticks consumed 3 or 4 amperes. Today the electrochemist operates furnaces utilizing more than 250,000 amperes and enough electrical energy to run all the industries and to light all the homes in a fair-sized American town. This comparison shows the progress which has been made in applying the electrochemical processes of an electric furnace to modern industry.

The chemist's control over many of the materials of nature was long limited by the range of temperatures at his command. He could not stir up any hotter fires on a commercial scale than could be furnished by burning coal, coke, or oil.

In the flame of an electric arc there is an inferno of nearly 7,000 degrees F. By enclosing an arc and putting it under an atmospheric pressure of 300 pounds per square inch, one can almost double the temperature of the electric flame. In such a place of torment, chemists can take apart defiant molecules that have resisted heat from other sources. In the same electric furnace, these molecules can be put together again in such new fashion as the chemist wishes. Many chemical reactions that cannot take place in fuel-fired furnaces occur rapidly in the electric furnace. When current generated by water power at low cost is available, these electrochemical processes are practical commercially.

Chapter Three

Useful Facts About Electricity FOR THE

YOUNG EXPERIMENTER IN ELECTROCHEMISTRY

Professor Ivan Andreyev, a talented scientist and a great teacher, once wrote in a letter to his pupils:

"Study, compare and accumulate facts. As perfect as is the structure of a bird's wing, the bird would never be able to fly if its wings were not supported by air. Facts are the air of the scientist; without them you would never be able to fly. Without them your theories are useless efforts."

Electrical terms are used frequently in the pages of this book. You can experiment with electrochemistry knowing little more than how to connect dry cells together in series. But a greater knowledge of electrical principles and of some of the terms used in electrical science will add greatly to the pleasure and understanding you will gain from your experiments. Here, for a few pages, are some facts about electricity.

WHAT IS ELECTRICITY?

Nowhere, neither here nor elsewhere, can you find an exact and satisfying answer to the question, "What is electricity?" No one, not even the most learned scientist, can give you a precise and full answer to that question. Electricity is the name of one of the fundamental quantities in nature. It is an invisible force, a form of energy which we cannot see. We are aware only of its effects, of the things that electricity does. This last statement is true of many things. For example, we cannot see the wind. We can see only the effects of the wind, such as ripples on a pond, ocean waves tumbling onto the shore, trees swaying, clouds scurrying, dust blowing, etc. In our experiments with electricity, we will never see electricity itself. We will be aware only of its effects, of the magnetism, heat, or light it produces, and of the chemical changes it brings about.

Present-day scientific opinion is that electricity consists of tiny invisible particles, all alike. They are called ELECTRONS. There are electrons present wherever matter exists. Matter is that of which any physical object is composed. A moving electron is an ELECTRIC CURRENT—a very feeble current, for it requires billions of moving electrons to produce a current of sufficient strength to do useful work. Approximately 5,240,093,717,045,500,000 electrons must move through the filament of the common 100-watt, 120-volt tungsten lamp each second in order to light it to full brilliance.

electricity produces magnetism, heat and light — and brings about chemical reactions

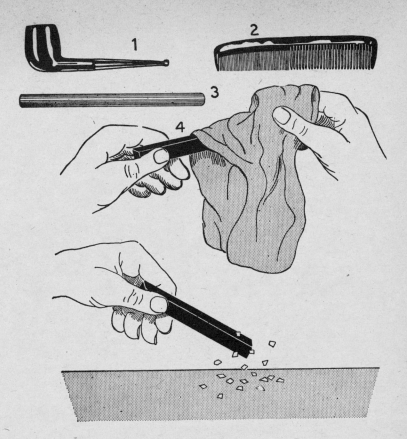

ELECTRONS

A moving stream of electrons is an electric current. An electric current is essential in all electrochemical processes. Electrons in the form of stationary charges, called STATIC electricity, first attracted the attention of scientists. A method of producing an electric current was discovered some time later. One method of producing static electricity is by friction. A number of common things will produce noticeable charges of static electricity when rubbed. A glass rod, a hard rubber pipestem, a stick of sealing wax, or a comb made of Lucite or rubber becomes charged when rubbed briskly with a piece of warm, dry woolen cloth or fur. An object thus charged will attract small bits of paper. Experiments with static electricity are not always successful in summer or during damp weather, because the static charge leaks away rapidly because of moisture in the air. Experiments with static electricity are performed best in winter when the air is dry.

ELECTRICITY CAN BE MEASURED

Almost everything that we deal with must be measured at some time. Food, time, money, distance, material substances, power and energy, all must be measured. Measuring is simply the comparison of something with a known standard. There are things which we cannot see but which we can measure. Time cannot be seen, but it can be measured in seconds, minutes, hours, days, weeks, months, years, decades, and centuries. Light can be measured in LUMENS, heat in CALORIES, energy in ERGS, FOOT-POUNDS, and HORSE-POWER, radio wave lengths in METERS, and so forth.

Electricity cannot be measured by the standards used to measure anything else. An inch, an ounce, a gram, a

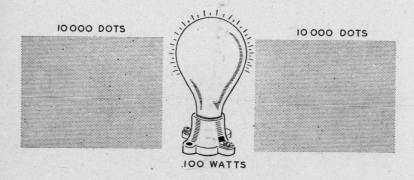

10 000 DOTS   10 000 DOTS

.100 WATTS

5,240,093,717,045,500,000 *ELECTRONS*

Approximately that number of electrons must pass through the filament of the common 100-watt, 120-volt tungsten filament lamp every second to light it to full brilliance. There are 20,000 dots in the two shaded rectangles above. Approximately 262 trillion times as many electrons are required every second to light such a lamp as there are dots in the rectangles.

calorie will not do it. The only way of measuring electricity is by some of the effects which it produces. Its chemical, heating, or electromagnetic effects must be used as its standard of measurement.

The two units used most frequently in measuring electricity are the AMPERE and the VOLT. The simplest way to explain the ampere and volt is to say that the amperage of a current of electricity represents its VOLUME and that the voltage indicates its force, or PRESSURE. Voltage, potential, and electromotive force of an electric current all mean the same thing. Calling voltage PRESSURE and amperage VOLUME is not entirely accurate, but neither is it a wholly inaccurate comparison. However, this definition will serve until you have progressed in science far beyond the pages of this book.

The Ampere

The first method of measuring an electric current was a chemical one, a device whereby the EFFECT of an electric current could be weighed and the amount of current which passed calculated. The current was sent through a solution of copper sulfate by means of two copper plates, or electrodes, which were dipped into the solution after having been accurately weighed. When the current had flowed for a time, the copper plates were taken out of the solution and weighed. One plate had increased in weight. Copper had been deposited on one of the plates by ELECTROCHEMICAL action. The amount of electric current which will deposit 1.777 grams of copper in 1 hour is called 1 AMPERE. The ampere, a unit of elec-

ampere — amount; quantity

tric current measurement which implies quantity or amount, was named in honor of André Marie Ampère, a French scientist who discovered many useful facts about electric current.

Thomas A. Edison employed this simple method of measuring the amount of electric current consumed by customers of the famous Edison Pearl Street Electric

 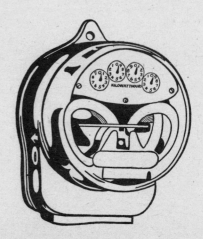

THE FIRST ELECTRIC LIGHT METER WAS AN ELECTROCHEMICAL DEVICE

Thomas A. Edison utilized the electrochemical action of an electric current to measure the amount of power consumed by each customer of the Edison Electric Light Company. His meter consisted of a pair of zinc plates (*see left-hand sketch*) immersed in a solution of zinc sulfate. A known portion of the current used by the customer passed through the solution. Once a month the zinc plates were removed and weighed. The change in their weight indicated how much current had been used, and a bill was rendered accordingly. Compare this first electric light meter with the direct-reading wattmeter (*see right-hand sketch*) in your home. Here is an indication of the great progress which has been made in electrical science in less than a generation.

Lighting Station in New York City. This was the first public utility electrical generating station in America. The customer's meter consisted of two zinc plates immersed in a solution of zinc sulfate contained in a glass jar. A certain known portion of the current used on the premises passed through this meter. Once a month the zinc plates were removed and others left in their place. The plates which had been removed were taken back to the Edison plant and weighed on a chemical balance. A bill was made out and sent to the customer for the amount of energy used, calculated on the basis of the amount of zinc deposited on one of the plates by the electrochemical action of the electric current.

The Volt and the Ohm

RESISTANCE. One way to comprehend certain things about an electric current is to compare it to a stream of water flowing through a pipe. In order for water to flow through a pipe, it must have pressure behind it. You can feel the pressure of a stream of water if you try to shut off the water running from a faucet by holding your thumb over the outlet.

The pressure of a stream of water enables it to overcome the friction the water meets in rubbing against the walls of the pipe in which it is moving. It is pressure which forces water through small openings, around turns, and upward against the force of gravity. In other words, pressure overcomes RESISTANCE, which a stream of water must overcome in order to move through a pipe.

An electric current also meets with resistance as it

moves through a wire or through a chemical solution. The amount of resistance will depend upon the size, the length, and the material of which the wire is made, or on the amount and nature of the substances in solution. Small wires offer more resistance than large wires. Wires made of aluminum, iron, nickel, or tungsten have more resistance than wires of equal size made of copper or silver. Silver has less resistance than copper, but it costs more, and copper and aluminum are the most practical materials to use in leading an electric current from one place to another.

THE VOLT AND THE OHM.   In order for an electric current to force its way through the resistance which it meets in moving through a conductor, it must have pressure, or, to use the appropriate electrical term, VOLTAGE. The volt is the measuring unit of electrical pressure. It is named after Alessandro Volta, the same Italian scientist who devised the first battery.

volt = pressure A volt may be measured in several ways by the effects it produces. It is most easily measured by the amount of *amount* electric current, or amperage, it will force through a certain amount of resistance. Electrical resistance for direct currents, that is, currents which flow constantly in one direction, is measured in OHMS. This unit of measurement is named after Georg Simon Ohm, the German physicist who discovered the laws of resistance. The standard ohm, called the international ohm,* is the re-

* On January 1, 1948, the "international" system of electrical units was abandoned and the "absolute" system universally adopted. The absolute ohm is the standard ohm in the United States. 1.000495 absolute ohms equals 1 international ohm.

sistance offered to an electric current by a column of pure mercury having a cross section of 1 square millimeter and a length of 106.28 centimeters at a temperature of 0 degrees Centigrade.

Having a unit of resistance, it is simple to measure voltage. The electrical pressure (electromotive force) which will force sufficient current through a circuit having a resistance of 1 ohm to deposit 1.777 grams of copper on an electrode in a period of 1 hour is a VOLT. Or, to put it differently, a volt is the electrical pressure which will force a current of 1 ampere through a resistance of 1 ohm. A flashlight cell has an electromotive force of about 1.5 volts. The pressure of the house-lighting current is usually about 120 volts, or eighty times that of a single flashlight cell. Consequently, the 120 volts can force eighty times as many amperes through a resistance as a single flashlight cell can.

Voltmeters and Ammeters

Fortunately, it is no longer necessary to pass a current through a solution and weigh the electrodes, as Edison did, to measure current flow. Direct-reading instruments called volt meters, ammeters, and wattmeters are available and will show instantly, on a scale, how much current is flowing at what voltage and will also indicate the total amount of energy. Milliammeters and millivoltmeters measure THOUSANDTHS of an ampere or volt. Microammeters and microvoltmeters measure MILLIONTHS of an ampere or volt. Resistance values may be measured in a few seconds by a direct-reading instru-

milli – thousandths
micro – millionths
kilo – thousands
mega – millions

AMMETER   **VOLTMETER**

amount, volume   *EMF; pressure*

METERS FOR MEASURING ELECTRICITY

Two qualities of an electric current can be measured by direct-reading instruments called ammeters and voltmeters. An ammeter indicates the number of amperes flowing; a voltmeter indicates the electromotive force, or voltage, of the current.

ment called an ohmmeter or with a device called a "bridge" (short for Wheatstone bridge).

Whenever it is necessary to indicate either fractions or very large values of the ampere, volt, and ohm, it is customary to use the prefixes MILLI, MICRO, KILO, and MEG as follows:

$$\text{millivolt} \quad = \frac{1}{1,000} \text{ of a volt}$$

$$\text{milliampere} = \frac{1}{1,000} \text{ of an ampere}$$

$$\text{microvolt} \quad = \frac{1}{1,000,000} \text{ of a volt}$$

$$\text{microampere} = \frac{1}{1,000,000} \text{ of an ampere}$$

kilovolt   = 1,000   volts

kiloampere   = 1,000   amperes

megohm   = 1,000,000 ohms

The Coulomb and the Watt

There are other units of electrical measurement besides the ampere, volt, and ohm, but only two with which the young experimenter in electrochemistry need concern himself. They are the WATT and the COULOMB. A watt is the unit of electrical POWER. You will often see this word or its initial, "W," stamped on the name plate of electrical devices. If you know how many watts an electric motor, a lamp, or a radio uses, you know how much energy is required to operate it.

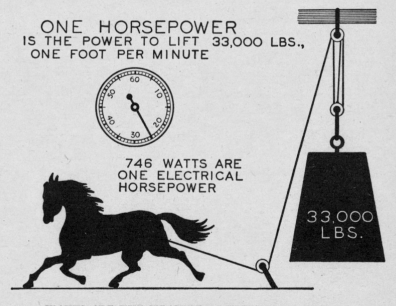

ONE HORSEPOWER
IS THE POWER TO LIFT 33,000 LBS.,
ONE FOOT PER MINUTE

746 WATTS ARE
ONE ELECTRICAL
HORSEPOWER

33,000
LBS.

WATTS ARE THE MEASURE OF ELECTRICAL ENERGY
In a direct current circuit, the product of the voltage multiplied by the number of amperes flowing indicates the WATTS, or units of electrical energy.

ampere × *voltage* = *electrical energy* DC
AMOUNT · · · PRESSURE · · WATTS consumed

The unit of power called a WATT is the energy represented by a current of 1 ampere having a potential of 1 volt. In the case of a direct current, the number of watts consumed in a circuit is found by multiplying the amperes by the volts. If an electric iron uses 5 amperes at 120 volts, it consumes 5 × 120, or 600 watts.

So far none of the measuring units which have been mentioned have taken time into consideration. Time is a very important element whenever energy is being considered. The electrical measuring unit called the COULOMB involves time.

One ampere flowing for ONE SECOND is the unit called a coulomb. One ampere flowing for one hour is called an AMPERE HOUR. Time also may enter into consideration in connection with the watt. One watt flowing for one hour is a WATT HOUR, and one kilowatt flowing for one hour is a KILOWATT HOUR.

ALTERNATING AND DIRECT CURRENT

Alternating current is often called A.C. and direct current is spoken of as D.C.

An alternating current changes its direction of flow at regular intervals. The electric current which comes into our homes from a public utility generating station to furnish light and power is almost without exception an alternating current which changes its direction of flow 120 times per second. It is said to have a frequency of 60 cycles. Alternating electric current for light and power is produced by a special type of dynamo called an ALTER-

NATOR. When an alternating current has passed from zero
to its maximum in one direction, died away to zero, risen
to a maximum in the opposite direction, and gone back
to zero again, it has completed one CYCLE. There are two
ALTERNATIONS per cycle.

A direct current does not change its direction of flow
at regular intervals, but flows constantly in the same
direction. Batteries and dynamos produce direct current.
Alternating currents may be changed into direct currents
by devices called RECTIFIERS.

In electrochemical work, direct current is necessary for
the process called ELECTROLYSIS. Electric furnaces are
operated usually on alternating current.

Chapter Four

Ions, Traveling Atoms, and Groups of Traveling Atoms

As previously mentioned, in the history of chemical discovery we often find a young man solving a problem which has baffled older and more experienced men. Davy and Berzelius were two such young men. Now we come to the third of an immortal trio, Svante Arrhenius.

Svante Arrhenius was a college student at the time that he devised what is today one of the most useful implements of the chemist, namely the Ionization Theory. The Ionization Theory is also known by the rather imposing title of The Theory of Electrolytic Dissociation. In spite of its bewildering names, the theory is merely an explanation of invisible occurrences in certain solutions. It works so well in practice that it is perhaps more than a theory. There is usually a bit of speculation involved in a theory, but the principles of the

Ionization Theory are undoubtedly facts. It explains, for example:

1. why some substances, namely those chemical compounds called ACIDS, BASES, and SALTS, conduct an electric current when dissolved in water, whereas others do not;

2. why substances whose solutions conduct electric current are decomposed by it, whereas substances whose solutions do not conduct the electric current are not decomposed.

PURE WATER DOES NOT CONDUCT
ELECTRIC CURRENT WELL

Quite contrary to the general belief among those who are not chemists, water itself is not a good conductor of electricity. We will see why in a moment, and we will also see the reason for this erroneous belief.

Only a very small electric current can pass through distilled water. The conductivity of pure water is very slight. Neither does DRY salt (sodium chloride) offer a good path to an electric current. But if a small amount of salt is dissolved in distilled water, a strong electric current can pass through the SOLUTION.

The student Arrhenius sought the reason for such phenomena by experimenting. He shut himself up in his laboratory and, day after day, night after night, filled beaker after beaker with solutions of different salts, testing each one to see if it would conduct an electric current. At the same time he was constantly using the "eye of his mind."

Svante Arrhenius was a dreamer. His thoughts soared in the clouds at times as he puttered with his tubes and beakers. He began to have some novel ideas of his own to explain why an electric current passes through some solutions but not through others. For two years he toiled ceaselessly. Amid the never-ending experiments with solutions of more than fifty different salts in all possible degrees of dilution, and the ceaseless, painstaking washing of bottles and beakers, he pondered the meaning of it all. Suddenly during the night of May 17, 1883, the answer to the great riddle flashed into the mind of the intrepid young experimenter.

Arrhenius decided that when a solid salt like common table salt is dissolved in water, an invisible event occurs. Some of the MOLECULES of sodium chloride SPLIT UP when they enter the solution and go swimming around in the water absolutely free from other atoms with which they were formerly joined. Some of the sodium and some of the chlorine atoms are no longer in partnership in the form of salt molecules. These broken molecules do not split into ATOMS of chlorine and ATOMS of sodium but into IONS of chlorine and IONS of sodium.

THE DIFFERENCE
BETWEEN AN ATOM AND AN ION

Atoms are not ions and ions are not atoms. Atoms and ions differ from each other in that atoms are neutral and do not bear an electrical charge. "Ion" is the Greek word for "traveler." Ions, in a chemist's language, are not only atoms or groups of atoms which carry an electrical charge, but they are travelers. Later, in experimenting with electrolysis, we will learn how ions travel toward the electrodes of an electrolytic cell. The presence of the electrical charge which changes an atom or a group of atoms into an ion also changes the physical properties and the chemical behavior of the atom.

Today chemists accept the explanation offered by Arrhenius. The amazing splitting or dissociation which is part of his theory apparently occurs whenever an acid, a salt, or a base dissolves in water. Arrhenius' theory put chemistry on a new foundation and gave us a better understanding of electrochemical processes.

The Electron Theory and the Ionization Theory make it possible to draw a helpful diagram of the way in which the elements sodium and chlorine combine to form

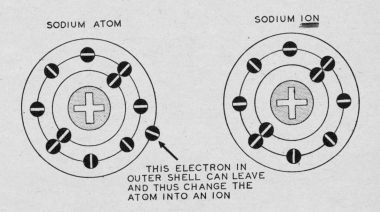

SODIUM ATOM   SODIUM ION

THIS ELECTRON IN OUTER SHELL CAN LEAVE AND THUS CHANGE THE ATOM INTO AN ION

HOW AN ATOM BECOMES AN ION, AND VICE VERSA

A single electron in the outer shell of an atom of the metallic elements can leave the atom and change it into an ion which bears a positive charge and is called an anion. When the ion regains an electron, it loses its charge and becomes an atom again.

sodium chloride, and how this compound dissociates into ions when it goes into solution in water.

For the benefit of those young experimenters who are interested in the "inner workings" of chemistry, a diagram showing the formation and the dissociation of sodium chloride is given.

An atom of sodium and an atom of chlorine are shown at the top of the diagram. The sodium atom, since it is a metal, has one "lonesome" electron in its outer ring which it is ready to lend to a non-metal atom or molecule. Chlorine is a non-metal. It has one vacant space in its outer ring and is therefore eager to borrow another electron from a metal atom. By moving together and sharing the "lonesome" electron, both atoms acquire complete outer rings and become the stable molecule called sodium chloride. So much for the formation of the molecule. Now let us see what happens when it dissociates.

When sodium chloride is dissolved in water, some of the salt molecules split into two parts, forming: a sodium ion, which is the original sodium atom now deprived of its "lonesome" electron and, consequently, positively charged; and a chlorine ion, which is the original chlorine atom now in possession of the "lonesome" electron and, consequently, negatively charged.

To understand how a sodium chloride molecule dissociates to form sodium and chlorine ions, one must know first how atoms of sodium and chlorine join to form sodium chloride. Chlorine has a vacant space for an electron in its outer shell. When an atom of sodium and an atom of chlorine move close to each other, the "lonesome" electron in the outer shell of the sodium atom fills the vacant space in the outer shell of the chlorine atom, as illustrated in diagrams on the opposite page.

THE FORMATION OF SODIUM CHLORIDE

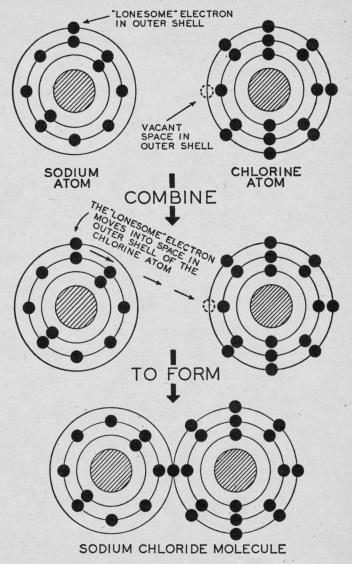

"LONESOME" ELECTRON
IN OUTER SHELL

VACANT
SPACE IN
OUTER SHELL

SODIUM
ATOM

CHLORINE
ATOM

COMBINE

THE "LONESOME" ELECTRON
MOVES INTO SPACE IN
OUTER SHELL OF THE
CHLORINE ATOM

TO FORM

SODIUM CHLORIDE MOLECULE

ELECTROLYTIC DISSOCIATION

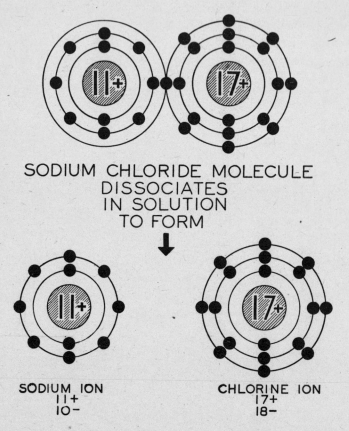

SODIUM CHLORIDE MOLECULE
DISSOCIATES
IN SOLUTION
TO FORM

SODIUM ION
11+
10−

CHLORINE ION
17+
18−

When sodium chloride dissolves in water, some of its molecules dissociate, that is, split apart and become sodium and chlorine IONS. A sodium chloride molecule thus splits into a positively charged sodium ion (a sodium atom minus its "lonesome" electron) and a negatively charged chloride ion (a chlorine atom with the vacant space in its outer shell occupied by an electron borrowed from a sodium atom).

The fact that ions carry an electrical charge helps to explain the electrochemical process called electrolysis.

ELECTROLYTES AND NON-ELECTROLYTES

Chemicals are classified and named according to their characteristic qualities.

An ELECTROLYTE is a substance which conducts an electric current and is decomposed by it WHEN IN SOLUTION.

A NON-ELECTROLYTE is a substance which, in solution, does not conduct a current of electricity.

Acids, Bases, and Salts Are Electrolytes

All acids, bases and salts are electrolytes. It is well to know exactly what is meant by the terms "acid," "base," and "salt."

The most common acids, those whose names are probably the most familiar, are the powerful and active sulfuric, nitric, and hydrochloric acids. Other common acids, weak in comparison to those just named, are citric, boric, lactic, and carbonic acids. There is a host of other acids whose names are familiar only to the chemist.

An acid is a compound which contains hydrogen that may be replaced by a metal when the acid and metal come into contact and whose water solution turns blue litmus paper red. An acid dissociates, or splits into ions, in a water solution. A water solution of an acid contains hydrogen atoms which are charged with positive electricity and are therefore hydrogen ions. Ions with a positive charge are called CATIONS and are so called because they travel to the CATHODE in electrolysis. A water solution of an acid contains negative ions as well as positive ions, or cations. Ions with a negative charge are called

ANIONS because they travel to the ANode during electrolysis. The nature of the anions formed from an acid depends upon the acid from which they are formed. The anions from an acid are often a GROUP of atoms carrying a negative charge. For example, the anions formed by the dissociation of sulfuric acid in water consist of an atom of sulfur and four atoms of oxygen. A sulfuric acid anion carries a double negative charge.

The important fact to remember about an acid is that every acid contains hydrogen, which comes out of the acid molecule when it meets a suitable metal and the metal takes its place. Not all metals can displace hydrogen from acids. Acids behave like acids only when they are in a water solution, at which time there are ions present.

A good illustration of the action of an acid and a metal is the preparation of the soldering acid which plumbers and tinsmiths use as a flux to clean the surfaces to be soldered so that the solder will adhere. This solution is often referred to as "killed acid." Pieces of zinc are dropped into a strong solution of hydrochloric acid in water. A rapid chemical reaction occurs. Zinc displaces the hydrogen in the acid molecule. You can see the hydrogen escaping in the form of bubbles in the solution. When the hydrochloric acid has its hydrogen atom displaced by zinc, the product that remains is zinc chloride.

Definitions can be very tiresome, but if you wish to understand some of the fundamental chemical processes, you will need to know what a BASE is. Bases are an important class of chemical compounds. When an acid and a base are mixed together, the reaction between them produces a useful chemical compound called a SALT.

A base is usually a combination of a metallic element with one or more groups of atoms called HYDROXYL GROUPS. A hydroxyl is an atom of hydrogen in partnership with an atom of oxygen. The partnership is an important one in chemistry. It results in many useful hydroxides, such as lye, milk of magnesia, limewater, household ammonia, and aluminum hydroxide.

Ammonia presents another aspect of the term "base." The word "usually" was used in the definition of a base in order to give a simple, temporary definition. Now we must add to it by explaining that although a base is usually a combination of a metal with one or more hydroxyl groups, there are some NON-METALS which form bases. These particular non-metals have the trick of acting like metals. Ammonia is one of them. Ammonia is not a metal; it is a gas which consists of one atom of nitrogen in a molecule with three atoms of hydrogen. If compressed sufficiently, ammonia gas becomes a liquid.

A water solution of a base always contains pairs of hydrogen and oxygen groups in the form of hydroxyl ions carrying a charge of negative electricity. A water solution of a base turns red litmus paper blue.

Experiments with Electrolytes and Non-electrolytes

The four experiments which follow in this chapter require the use of the 120-volt house-lighting current. They are intended for use as demonstrations by science teachers and older students who are able to handle the apparatus with intelligence and care. Anyone who touches both carbon electrodes at the same time, when the apparatus is plugged in, will receive a shock—probably not a severe one because there are two lamps in the circuit whose resistance reduces the voltage and current. Also the contact area of the electrodes is small. A shock is unpleasant and frightening to some persons. *The apparatus used for these experiments is not dangerous but the 120-volt alternating house-lighting current can be. The apparatus should not be plugged into an outlet until it is ready for use. As soon as the experiments are finished the plug should be pulled out of the socket, so that the apparatus is disconnected from the power source.*

You can prove to your own satisfaction that pure water and several other liquids are not good conductors of electric current. You will need to arrange two 15-watt, 120-volt tungsten lamps in series with two carbon or graphite electrodes and connect the arrangement to the house-lighting current. The circuit is arranged so that the lamps light only when a conducting path is provided between the electrodes. The carbon or graphite rods (from size D flashlight cells) are supported in two holes in a wooden bracket arranged so that they can be immersed in a liquid contained in an 8-ounce glass beaker or tumbler. The details and dimensions of the support for the rods are shown in the illustration on the next page. The circuit is also illustrated (page 46).

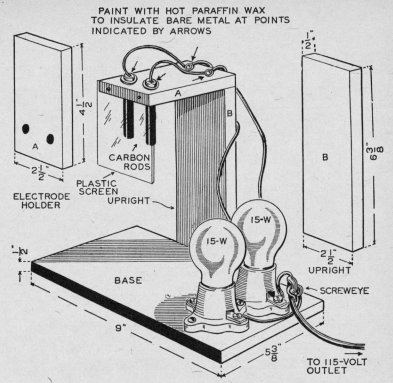

PAINT WITH HOT PARAFFIN WAX
TO INSULATE BARE METAL AT POINTS
INDICATED BY ARROWS

***HOMEMADE APPARATUS FOR DETERMINING ELECTROLYTES
AND NON-ELECTROLYTES***

Two 15-watt, 120-volt incandescent lamps, two porcelain lamp sockets, wire, screweye, two carbon rods from size D flashlight cells, and three pieces of ½-inch plywood are needed to construct this apparatus. In a laboratory, platinum wires would be used as electrodes, but platinum is too costly for the average amateur experimenter. The carbon rods must be boiled in hot water and thoroughly rinsed to remove the sal ammoniac (ammonium chloride) and zinc chloride which may have penetrated the carbon. Otherwise these salts might go into solution in the distilled water which is to be used in an experiment. The water would then be impure and the experiment spoiled.

Connection can be made to each rod by soldering a copper wire to the brass cap. Use rosin-cored solder or rosin as the flux, in order to avoid the chemical contamination which might result from using soldering acid or paste.

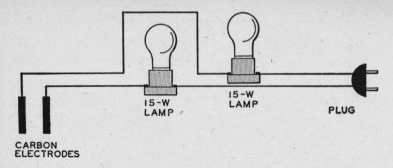

CARBON
ELECTRODES

CIRCUIT FOR THE APPARATUS SHOWN IN THE PREVIOUS ILLUSTRATION

The lamps are screwed into two sockets (called flat-base porcelain receptacles) fastened to the wooden base. Two 15-watt, 120-volt lamps are used because lamps of this small size have more resistance than larger lamps and limit the current more. One lamp is placed in each leg of the circuit. There is a reason for this. One wire of the 120-volt house-lighting system is always connected to the ground when the wiring is installed. The other wire (ungrounded) is called the "hot" wire by electricians and it is only necessary to touch this ONE wire to receive a shock if your person is also grounded. You are grounded while standing on a concrete floor, touching a radiator, touching an electric fixture or appliance, etc. When an 120-volt, 15-watt lamp is placed in each leg of the circuit, the current is reduced, so that if the ground and the "hot" side of the circuit were touched simultaneously the shock would not be dangerous.

The lamps and electrodes are connected together with rubber-covered lamp cord. The power cord is anchored to a screw eye in the wood base to relieve the connections from strain. The wires are connected to the carbon electrodes by soldering to the brass caps on the upper ends.

EXPERIMENT *showing that pure water is not a good conductor of electric current.* Plug the cord connected to the lamp and carbon rods into a convenient 120-volt house-lighting outlet. When you hold the blade of a knife or screwdriver against the electrodes, it will complete the lamp circuit and the lamp should light.

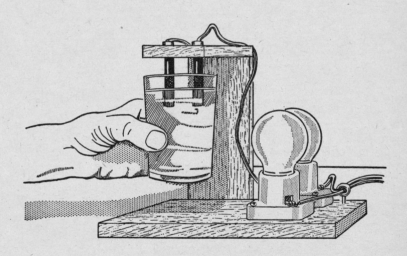

PURE WATER IS NOT A GOOD CONDUCTOR OF ELECTRIC CURRENT

The lamps fail to light when the carbon electrodes are immersed in distilled water. The reason: there are very few ions present.

Fill a clean 8-ounce glass tumbler with distilled water and bring it up under the electrodes until they are both immersed in the water. The lamp will fail to light. A good path of low resistance is not provided by the distilled water. Not enough current can pass to light the lamp. You can safely conclude that pure water is not a good conductor of electric current. There is, of course, a reason. The reason is that THERE ARE VERY FEW IONS present in pure water.

Other Non-conductors

EXPERIMENT.   Try another experiment, using, in place of distilled water, some alcohol mixed with distilled water. Try also solutions of cane sugar made by dissolving sugar in distilled water. If you can get some pure glycerine, mix some with distilled water. Immerse the carbon electrodes in all three of these solutions. In each case the lamps will fail to light. The solutions will prove to be non-conductors of electricity, or non-electrolytes. The lamps will fail to light for the same reason that they failed to light in the experiment with distilled water. There are not enough ions present in these solutions to conduct sufficient current across the solution between the carbon rods to light the lamp.

An Electrolyte Dissolved in Pure Water
Conducts a Current of Electricity

EXPERIMENT.   Dissolve a teaspoonful of table salt (sodium chloride) in an 8-ounce glass tumbler or beaker which is almost filled with distilled water. Bring the salt solution up under the electrodes so that they are im-

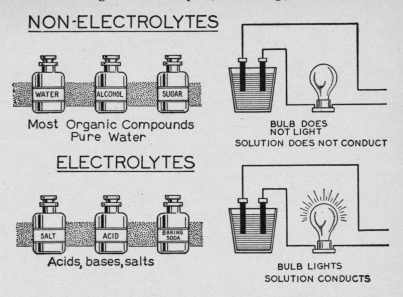

NON-ELECTROLYTES

Most Organic Compounds
Pure Water

BULB DOES NOT LIGHT
SOLUTION DOES NOT CONDUCT

ELECTROLYTES

Acids, bases, salts

BULB LIGHTS
SOLUTION CONDUCTS

AN ELECTROLYTE DISSOLVED IN DISTILLED WATER IS A GOOD CONDUCTOR .

The lamps light when the carbon electrodes are immersed in a solution of sodium chloride, washing soda, or other electrolyte. The electrolytes provide ions.

mersed in it. The lamps will light, indicating that there is a conducting path between the electrodes and that the circuit is completed. Salt is an electrolyte. When it goes into solution in water, ions are formed. It is by means of the electrical charges on the ions that an electric current is able to pass through the salt solution.

Other Common Electrolytes

EXPERIMENT. Sal ammoniac (ammonium chloride), washing soda (sodium carbonate), baking soda (sodium bicarbonate), Epsom salts (magnesium sulfate), and vinegar (dilute acetic acid) are common electrolytes. They all furnish ions, and their solutions are good conductors of electric current. Some of these substances may be found in the kitchen cupboard, and you can prove that they are electrolytes by dissolving any of them in distilled water and testing the solution with the lamp and electrodes.

OTHER INTERESTING FACTS
ABOUT SOLUTIONS

All the molecules of an electrolyte do not always dissociate immediately and become ions when they go into solution. The number of molecules which split up depends upon the electrolyte, the solvent, the temperature, the concentration, and any other ions which may be present. Water is the only common solvent in which ionization takes place. Alcohols, benzene, lacquer thinner, turpentine, and most of the other solvents are not ionizing solvents.

Dissolving a substance in a liquid raises the boiling point and lowers the freezing point of the liquid. Sugar dissolved in water lowers the freezing point below 32 degrees F and raises the boiling point above 212 degrees F.

A given number of molecules of a non-electrolyte such as sugar or glycerine, dissolved in a given quantity of water, will raise the boiling point of the water a fixed amount, and this amount is always the same no matter which non-electrolyte is used. In other words, if 10 molecules of sugar are dissolved in 500 molecules of pure water, or 10 molecules of glycerine are dissolved in 500 molecules of water, the boiling point of each solution will be raised the same amount.

You may be surprised when you learn what happens in the case of electrolytes under the same circumstances. Ten molecules of table salt (sodium chloride) dissolved in 500 molecules of water will raise the boiling point TWICE as much as 10 molecules of sugar or glycerine dissolved in 500 molecules of water. Ten molecules of sodium sulfate dissolved in 500 molecules of water will raise the boiling point nearly three times as much as will 10 molecules of sugar or glycerine.

The Ionization Theory of Svante Arrhenius explains this interesting phenomenon. It makes clear that the lowering of the freezing point and the raising of the boiling point of water is PROPORTIONAL to the NUMBER and not the KIND of particles dissolved in it. Non-electrolytes such as sugar and glycerine do not dissociate when they go into solution. Ten molecules of these substances remain ten molecules of sugar or glycerine or whatever other non-electrolyte they may be. On the other hand, electrolytes dissociate. A molecule of sodium chloride consists of one atom of sodium and one atom of chlorine. Ten molecules of sodium chloride are 10 particles but become 20 ions (10 sodium ions and 10 chlorine ions) or TWICE as many particles when they ionize in 500 molecules of water. Each molecule of sodium sulfate contains TWO atoms of sodium. Ten molecules of sodium

Na₂(SO₄)

sulfate are 10 particles but in water become 30 particles because they ionize into 20 sodium ions and 10 sulfate ions, or THREE times as many particles. A similar process of reasoning, said young Arrhenius, explains the action of electrolytes in lowering the freezing point. Clever young man, was he not?

Electrolytes may be divided into the following classes:

A. STRONG ELECTROLYTES: These substances may be regarded as being 100 per cent ionized.

ACIDS: Hydrochloric, nitric, sulfuric, chloric, perchloric, hydrobromic, hydriodic, permanganic

BASES: The hydroxides of potassium, sodium, calcium, strontium, barium, magnesium, lithium

SALTS: Nearly all salts, with the exception of some mercury and some cadmium and lead salts

B. MODERATELY STRONG ELECTROLYTES:

ACIDS: Acetic, nitrous, phosphoric, oxalic, hydrofluoric, sulfurous

BASES: Ammonium hydroxide, silver hydroxide (only slightly soluble in water). The hydroxides of copper, cadmium, nickel, zinc, ferrous iron, cobalt, and manganese are not soluble in water, and their degree of ionization is not known.

SALTS: Lead acetate, mercuric chloride

C. WEAK ELECTROLYTES:

ACIDS: Carbonic, boric, hypochlorous, hypocyanic

BASES: Hydroxides of aluminum, ferric iron, mercury, chromium, bismuth

SALTS: Mercuric cyanide

Chapter Five

Niagara Falls, the First Center of Electrochemical Industry

The tumbling waters of the Niagara River generated the first low-cost electrical power. This power made many electrochemical processes commercially practical, enterprises which could not have endured if they had been dependent upon higher-cost, steam-generated power. Consequently, the City of Niagara Falls and its environs became a center of electrochemical industry. The history of power development at Niagara is an interesting story.

THE DISCOVERY OF NIAGARA FALLS

About a hundred years before the thirteen American colonies fought their War of Independence and became the United States of America—in the year 1679, to be exact—a stalwart missionary pushed his way through the trackless wilderness around the western part of the lake now called Ontario. No European had been in this area before. The missionary, whose name was Father Hennepin, had left his home in Belgium to explore the new country and to carry on missionary work among the Iroquois Indians. His travels had taken him as far west as the site of the present city of Peoria, Illinois. He was accustomed to hardship and adventure. He expected to see many new and strange things in this new land, but on this particular day he had happened upon something which he had never experienced. He could not see it, he could only hear it. A deep, far-off roar filled the air on all sides. It grew louder as he walked along. Usually the forest was silent, unless rain was falling or the wind was blowing. But today the sky was clear and there was no wind in the trees. What could be the cause of this strange sound which drew him on until it seemed very close? He finally stepped through a screen of thick bushes, stopped, and caught his breath. He stood on the brink of a deep chasm, looking at one of the wonders of the world. There before the astonished eyes of Father Hennepin a mighty river was tumbling over a high cliff. The breathless missionary and explorer for the King of France was looking at Niagara Falls, and history tells us that he was the first European to do so.

The magnificence of the great falls at Niagara has probably attracted more visitors than any other work of nature in America. The falls are a scenic wonder which people from all over the world travel to see. But the great cataract, the scenery, and the sightseers are incidental in the story of electrochemistry. Niagara Falls' greatest service has been more than that of providing a spectacle of grandeur. The tremendous development of water power for generating low-cost electric power by United States and Canadian companies at Niagara Falls is of international importance. Here are many industries, born of the union of electrical power with chemistry, turning out electrochemical products which have be-

THE DISCOVERY OF NIAGARA FALLS

The first European to see Niagara Falls was Father Hennepin, a Franciscan Recollect missionary, who came to North America from Belgium to carry on missionary work among the Iroquois Indians and to explore the new country. He discovered Niagara Falls in 1679.

Low-cost hydroelectric power first produced at the Falls made Niagara the birthplace of commercial electrochemistry. (From *The Boys' Book of Motors, Engines and Turbines,* by Alfred Morgan)

come important factors in our national wealth, health, and comfort. At Niagara Falls we can find factories bearing such well-known names as The Aluminum Company of America, The Carborundum Company, The Union Carbide and Carbon Corporation, The Norton Company, The Mathiewson Alkali Company, The American Cyanamid Company, The Hooker Electrochemical Company, and a host of others. If we look inside these manufactories, we will hear the hum of transformers and motor-generators, see the brilliant flashing of electric arcs, see glowing furnaces filled with molten metals and long rows of silent electrochemical cells. Niagara Falls is the center of the electrochemical industry.

The Power at Niagara

The overflow from Lake Erie runs through the Niagara River to Lake Ontario. The river drops 326 feet in approximately 26 miles between the lakes. Nearly all this drop occurs within 5 miles of Niagara Falls. The Falls themselves are over 160 feet high. More than 93,000,000 gallons of water flow from one lake to another each minute of the twenty-four hours. In the vast power contained in these falling waters was a challenge for men to utilize it, an invitation to engineers to harness it to their wheels in its hurry to the sea.

For many years this challenge had to go unanswered. A little water was taken, to be sure, from the rapids above the American Falls and allowed to tumble over old-fashioned water wheels. But the real power of the river went past unharnessed. When powerful turbines and large generators at last were built, the river was conquered, and the development of water power at Niagara became a model for the rest of the world.

On the American side, the power developed is more than 600,000 horsepower, generated by two plants. The Canadian Fall is larger than the American Fall. It generates 874,700 horsepower in three plants at or near the Fall and 121,000 horsepower in a fourth plant some distance away. The total amount of power developed at Niagara Falls is, therefore, about 1,500,000 horsepower. The service of Niagara extends to every city and town in the country in the form of the highly valuable industrial processes carried on near the Falls by means of the electric power generated by the falling water. These processes can be carried on only where low-cost electricity can be generated and long wires are unnecessary. When it is unnecessary to build an expensive dam and to flood large areas of land, electricity can be generated at lower cost by harnessing water power than by burning oil or coal. The river's ceaseless supply of energy makes possible the great factories at Niagara which produce aluminum, Carborundum for grinding tools and metal surfaces, chemicals for purifying drinking water and bleaching cloth, alloys indispensable for modern steelmaking, and many other materials. Farther along in this book is a list of the products of the electric furnace and the electrolytic cell; the list fills nearly three pages.

Niagara's First Power Development

The first man, so far as we know, to use the waters

of the Niagara River for power was Chabert Joncaire, a French fur trader who lived on the bank of the river not far from the Falls. Joncaire decided to set up a small sawmill and use some of the power which was rushing past his doorstep and going to waste. In 1757 he carried out his plan. He dug a ditch which took water from the rapids above the American Fall and led it along the bank for a short distance. Here the water poured down upon a wooden wheel and returned to the river. The turning mill wheel was used to drive Joncaire's crude sawmill. If you visit Niagara Falls, you may see a duplicate of Joncaire's ditch at the site of the original.

This first attempt to use the Niagara River for power had hardly been completed before war came to the river's banks. Great Britain and France were in armed conflict, and the British drove the French settlers out. Then the American Revolutionary army swept the British troops from the river. Peace, when it arrived, did not stay long. Soon England and her former colonies were plunged into the war of 1812. British troops burned to the ground the city of Buffalo, New York, at the head of the Niagara River. Bloody battles were fought at Lundy's Lane and Chippawa, within sound of Niagara's roaring waters. History was made during those years, but it was not the history of water power and manufacturing. The tremendous source of power that tumbled riotously over Niagara's cataracts was neglected.

When the war was over, men were able to turn their thoughts again to their homes, their businesses, and the things that make for the comfort and happiness of people in prosperity. The Porter family, which owned the land along the American rapids, invited men with money, and with the vision to see what the development of Niagara's water power would mean, to come there and aid in its development. In 1852 Caleb S. Woodhull and Walter Bryant accepted the invitation. They formed a company to dig a canal from the upper rapids to a point about a half-mile below the falls where it was planned to install huge water wheels. Unfortunately, the company which Woodhull and Bryant formed did not have enough money to continue to pay its workmen until the canal was completed. They had to abandon the project. Other men raised money and undertook to finish the canal. But they also failed. The Niagara River still remained unconquered.

WHITE COAL

It was not until 1879 that the dream of a power canal at the Falls came true. Jacob F. Schoellkopf, who had risen from a beginning as a poor immigrant boy to become a wealthy merchant and manufacturer in Buffalo, New York, became interested. In 1877 he bought the property of the last company that had attempted to dig the canal. Many shrewd men thought that he was making a mistake. The new company, with Schoellkopf at its head, went quietly to work enlarging and improving the old canal. The prophets of gloom were mistaken. By the year 1882, seven mills were using its water to drive their machinery.

dynamos produce direct current

At that time engineers had not used water wheels and turbines to drive dynamos. The first dynamos which would generate enough electric power to be of real practical use were not built until the year that Jacob Schoellkopf and his friends bought the old canal. The first practical dynamos (they were still small and crude machines) were built in 1877 and 1878 to supply electric current to operate arc lamps.

Arc lamps were one of the wonders of those days. An intense electric flame between two carbon rods produced a powerful, dazzling light which could be employed in factories, stores, and halls and was useful for street lighting. Thus, Davy's demonstration with the two pieces of charcoal and a battery found a practical application. Arc lamps proved to be too powerful and brilliant, and too unsteady, for use in the home. Their noisy and spluttering light has long since given way to silent and steady incandescent and fluorescent lamps. Arcs are used nowadays for irradiating milk and other foods and as "suntan" lamps, but no longer as a source of light for illumination.

arc = battery with carbon electrodes

In 1879 a small water wheel using water from the rapids above the falls at Niagara was used to drive one of the first lighting dynamos, and it supplied current for sixteen spluttering arc lamps in Prospect Park, Niagara Falls, New York. This new and amazing electrical wonder so interested people that the railroads ran excursion trains from all parts of the country to Niagara Falls in order that people might see this almost unbelievable sight. Today it is rather amusing to think of making a long journey to see an electric light, operated by water power from a river, illuminating a park by the river's side. But we must remember that many things which we consider to be quite ordinary did not exist one hundred years ago.

Jacob Schoellkopf and the men with whom he had surrounded himself in trying to develop the water power at Niagara were always ready to test new ideas. They decided to install a dynamo in a paper mill at Niagara Falls and to use the current to light the paper mill and any other buildings that might wish to install arc lamps. In 1881 this dynamo supplied the first electric power for public use ever generated by the tumbling water of Niagara. It was probably the first central electric station in the world. Soon after the dynamo was installed, it was suplying electricity for lighting a newspaper office, three factories, and three stores. With this small beginning, our era of great power development began. The wilderness which Father Hennepin had explored not so many years before was now occupied by fertile farms, busy cities, and prosperous towns. Railroads ran where deer paths and Indian trails had been. The lakes over which the canoe of the *voyageur* had moved were busy with a thousand ships.

But the greatest change was still to come. Electricity from Niagara was destined to make neighboring towns and cities into some of the world's greatest manufacturing centers. Niagara was to show the world how to use water power. The stage was set for some phenomenal electrochemical achievements.

THE FIRST CENTER
OF ELECTROCHEMICAL INDUSTRY

There was great interest in the new power plant at Niagara. The swift water rushing downgrade to Lake Ontario would produce electricity at lower cost than that produced by burning the dusty black coal of the mines. Electrochemical industry needs low-cost electric current twenty-four hours a day. Here it was. An industrial migration to Niagara Falls began; many new industries went there and set up their plants. Most of them are there today. Niagara Falls is still a great electrochemical industrial center from which come aluminum, carbide, Carborundum and other abrasives, ferroalloys, cyanamide, chlorine, sodium, caustic, and a host of other materials.

Electrochemical industries are to be found also at other points where hydroelectric power produces the required low-cost energy. At Massena, New York, where power is developed from the Long Sault Rapids of the St. Lawrence River, is the largest aluminum and carbide plant in the world. At Great Falls, Montana, in the center of a great copper and zinc mining district, are large copper and zinc refineries which purify metals by electricity. Factories near hydroelectric power stations in West Virginia produce ferroalloys, chlorine, caustic, and other products of electrochemistry. Steels and phosphoric acid are produced with the power developed at Anniston, Alabama.

Chapter Six

Some of the Processes
and Products of Electrochemistry

Knowledge of scientific facts and principles and their practical application make possible present-day rapid transportation and communication, the preservation and distribution of food, adequate sanitation, the cure of disease, etc. (The "etc." stands for a list of additional benefits which is so long it would be tiresome to read.)

No other agency has so greatly improved the economic, social, and intellectual life of mankind in an equal length of time. Electrochemical processes are an important portion of modern science. Help in providing our food is one of the many important things electrochemistry gives us.

THE WORLD'S NEED FOR NITROGEN

How Electrochemistry and the Atmosphere Supply Agriculture and Industry with an Essential Chemical

The atmosphere is approximately four-fifths NITROGEN by volume. Nitrogen is an essential in agriculture and in many industries. It must be added regularly to cultivated soil to restore and maintain the fertility of the soil. Nitrogen is a constituent of all living tissues. It is one of the principal foods required by plants. Stunted crops are produced by soils which are deficient in nitrogen.

There is a demand for large quantities of compounds containing nitrogen for the manufacture of nitric acid, dyes, drugs, explosives, synthetic fibers, plastics, and other products of the chemist's ingenuity. Natural nitrates found in large deposits in Chile were once the chemist's principal source of commercial nitrogen. Vast quantities were transported in ships from Chile to all parts of the world. The few known natural deposits of nitrogen are limited, and as the eventual exhaustion of such sources is inevitable, chemists gave thought to the immense reservoir of nitrogen in the atmosphere.

Nature is constantly converting, or FIXING, atmospheric nitrogen into compounds by natural processes. Bacteria of a type called nitrogen FIXERS, which are found in the roots of clover, soy, alfalfa, beans, and peas, change nitrogen into nitrates. Nitrates are compounds of nitrogen. Upon the death of the plants and their root bacteria, the nitrogen compounds break up and unite with elements in the soil, becoming available as plant food for the next crop.

Lightning is also a nitrogen fixer. Lightning has a purpose in the scheme of things and does not merely set fire to haystacks and strike flagpoles and church steeples. Every bolt of lightning that flashes across the sky causes small amounts of nitrogen and oxygen in the atmosphere to combine and form the compound called nitric oxide. The nitric oxide is immediately further oxidized into nitrogen peroxide. There is good evidence that nearly 400,000,000 tons of nitrogen is "fixed" every year by lightning during electrical storms. Much of this nitrogen peroxide dissolves in raindrops and snowflakes, enough, in fact, so that rain and snow deposit an average of about 6 pounds of nitrogen per acre on the earth's surface. Wherever it falls upon sand or soil, the fixed nitrogen forms food for plants. This amount of nitrogen (6 pounds per acre) is very small compared to that taken from the soil by crops.

Modern science, using nitrogen from the atmosphere as the basic raw material, has made the world independent of mineral deposits of nitrogen and provided a never-ending source of fertilizer and nitrogen compounds. The commercial process of converting the free nitrogen of the atmosphere into useful nitrogen compounds such as ammonia, nitric acid, and nitrates is called FIXATION of nitrogen. Nature's fixation processes are too slow to fill the agricultural and industrial demand for nitrogen compounds. More than one-half of the world's requirements of nitrogen compounds are now filled by fixation processes devised by chemists.

CYANAMID PROCESS. One of these processes produces a nitrogen compound called CYANAMIDE. In this process atmospheric nitrogen is passed over white hot calcium carbide. (The calcium carbide used in this process is produced by heating lime and coke in an electric furnace.) Ground calcium carbide is placed in iron drums which hold a charge of two tons and are fitted with pipe connections so that nitrogen may be fed in. To start the reaction the center of the charge is heated by means of an electrically heated carbon rod and the nitrogen turned on. The nitrogen is absorbed by the hot carbide and the reaction evolves so much heat that the carbon rod may be removed after a few minutes. A solid mass results which, after cooling, is crushed, powdered and sprayed with water to destroy any unchanged calcium carbide. The black powder resulting from the process is largely calcium cyanamide, a compound of calcium, carbon and nitrogen which is used in mixed fertilizers without further treatment.

The United States Government's nitrogen fixation plant at Muscles Shoals, Alabama employs the Cyanamid Process to produce nitrogen compounds for fertilizer and other purposes.

THE HABER PROCESS. The Haber Process is another method of utilizing the nitrogen in the atmosphere. That useful compound of hydrogen and nitrogen, called ammonia, results. A mixture of nitrogen and hydrogen are compressed to 3,000 pounds per square inch at a temperature of 900 degrees Fahrenheit in the presence of iron, which acts as a catalyst. About one-half of the nitrogen and hydrogen combine to form ammonia. Vast quantities of ammonia are required in industry.

A catalyst such as the iron used in the Haber Process alters the speed of a chemical reaction. The iron is a positive catalyst and speeds up the union of hydrogen and nitrogen. Berzelius proposed the name catalysis from a Greek word meaning *breaking down or decomposition*.

There are also negative catalysts which slow down or inhibit reactions.

Catalysis bears some of the aspects of an art rather than a science in spite of the many facts known about catalysts and catalytic reactions. Catalysis plays a great role in modern chemical manufacturing for it means the speeding up and cheapening of many processes.

In both the Cyanamid and Haber Fixation Processes electricity plays an essential part. In the Cyanamid Process an electric furnace furnishes the high temperature necessary to produce the required calcium carbide. Electricity also furnishes the heat to start the reaction between the nitrogen and carbide. In the Haber Process, the required hydrogen is often obtained by the electrolysis of water. Hydrogen from water-gas is used sometimes in the Haber Process but the ammonia which results contains more impurities than ammonia made from hydrogen obtained by the electrolysis of water. Water-gas is a mixture of carbon monoxide and hydrogen formed by heating coke with steam.

THE BIRKELAND-EYDE PROCESS. The simplest fixation process is the one which occurs in nature when a bolt of lightning forms nitrous oxides by combining oxygen and nitrogen in the atmosphere. This is the principle in the Birkeland-Eyde Process in Norway, where very low-cost hydroelectric power is available. Air, under pressure, is passed through a large electric arc. The purpose of the arc is to produce the very high temperature required for the combination of the nitrogen with oxygen. Nitric oxide is formed first. This converts immediately into nitrogen peroxide. Spraying and mixing the nitrogen peroxide with water produces weak nitric acid. Limestone is mixed with the weak nitric acid to form calcium nitrate—good fertilizer.

So, thanks to the electrochemist, when Chilean and other natural nitrate deposits are exhausted, we will be able to produce all the nitrogen compounds we need from the vast ocean of air surrounding us.

ALUMINUM

How Electrochemistry Changed a Curiosity into an Industrial Metal Second only to Steel in Volume of Production

When you unwrap the metal foil covering a piece of chocolate, or squeeze a tube of toothpaste, you are probably handling a piece of aluminum. When passed between heavy steel rollers, sheet aluminum can be squeezed out so thin that a pound of it will cover almost 500 square feet and be only 17 one-hundred-thousandths of an inch in thickness. Very thin sheet metal is called foil. Aluminum foil, as you are no doubt aware, is used as a wrapper for candy, cigarettes, gum, and a great variety of food products.

Pure aluminum is somewhat soft and weak. Research has shown that its strength can be increased greatly by the addition of small amounts of other metals such as copper, zinc, silicon, manganese and magnesium. The term "aluminum," when used in reference to the metal's industrial uses, serves as a generic name for a number of aluminum alloys. There are aluminum alloys which are stronger than structural steel.

Aluminum alloys have strength, light weight, and beauty. They have great resistance to corrosion and will not change the flavor, purity, or color of food. Railway coaches, bridge girders, window frames, airplanes, engine pistons, vacuum cleaners, boats, kitchen utensils, pins, nails, paint, and toothpaste tubes are made from aluminum alloys.

Among the important alloys of aluminum are two tough, light-weight metals called Duralumin and Magnalium. Duralumin was the first of the heat-treated, strong, wrought-aluminum alloys which provide an invaluable structural material for building aircraft. A German chemist, Alfred Wilm, invented Duralumin. He experimented for twelve years before he succeeded in producing it. The manufacture of Duralumin began in Germany shortly before the beginning of World War I. This was the metal which formed the framework of the Zeppelins which raided England. The Allies obtained pieces of the new alloy from a wrecked Zeppelin which fell to earth in France and succeeded in reproducing this amazing light-weight material before the end of the war.

Only a few of aluminum's many uses have been mentioned; actually it is employed in the construction of thousands of articles. Many aluminum articles are not immediately obvious. For example, the pistons in the cylinders of automobiles are usually made of aluminum alloy but are seen only by the manufacturer or by an engine mechanic when the engine is repaired. Aluminum pistons have only one-third the weight and, consequently, one-third the inertia of cast iron pistons of similar size. Parts of machinery which move back and forth or stop and start frequently, operate more smoothly and use less power if made of aluminum instead of iron or steel, because aluminum has less inertia.

Aluminum Wears a Disguise in Nature

Metallic aluminum, or "free" aluminum, as a geologist would call it, is never found in nature. It is always found in chemical combination with other elements. Aluminum makes up one-twelfth of the earth's crust, but it is always combined with other elements. Aluminum is the most plentiful element on earth next to oxygen and silicon. Nearly all common rocks and clays contain aluminum. It lies disguised in every clod. The clays are principally aluminum silicate. Mica and feldspar, two common minerals which are part of many rocks, are combinations of aluminum and silica. Many natural aluminum compounds are uninteresting, but several are romantic and precious. Several gem stones, among them the ruby, garnet, topaz, sapphire, and turquoise, are aluminum compounds.

Aluminum at $545 per Pound

In spite of the abundance of aluminum ore, the shining metal has been produced for little more than one hundred years. At first, aluminum metal was so scarce and costly to produce that it was the bauble of kings. It sold for $545 per pound and was more precious than gold. Hans Christian Oersted, Professor of Physics at the University of Copenhagen, Denmark, produced the first metallic aluminum in 1825.

Oersted was the scientist who discovered that an electric current produces magnetism. He obtained metallic aluminum in the form of a gray powder by reducing aluminum chloride with potassium and mercury. This process formed an aluminum amalgam. An amalgam is an alloy of one or more metals with mercury. When Oersted heated his amalgam to distill off the mercury, he obtained a gray aluminum powder.

Two years later, in 1827, Friedrich Wöhler, a young professor of chemistry at Göttingen, Germany, obtained metallic aluminum by the direct reduction of aluminum chloride with potassium. His aluminum was also in the form of a gray powder, and it was not until 1845 that he was able to transform the powder to solid metal, the particles of which were hardly larger than a pinhead. It was these small particles that first revealed aluminum's amazingly light weight.

There are interesting coincidences in the historical background of aluminum. The first occurred in 1854 when the French scientist, Henri Sainte-Claire Deville, and Robert Wilhelm von Bunsen, Professor of Chemistry at Heidelberg University, Germany, working independently of one another, discovered how to improve Wöhler's method of obtaining aluminum. They substituted sodium for potassium and found that large globules of metallic aluminum would appear in a fused mixture of aluminum chloride and sodium. Deville made a medal of his aluminum and presented it to Emperor Napoleon III. Napoleon saw many possibilities for the new light-weight metal and commissioned Deville to make aluminum helmets and armor for his French cuirassiers. Deville displayed several large bars of aluminum at the Paris Exposition in 1855, but aluminum armor was not manufactured in quantity until 1942.

During the period when aluminum cost more than gold, Napoleon's most honored guests were provided with forks and spoons of aluminum. Guests of less importance found gold forks and spoons at their place at the dinner table.

In 1855 Deville's aluminum sold for $100 per pound in Paris. Its cost was still so great that the metal could not be put to commercial use. It was still only a scientific curiosity, used in making rare jewelry and exhibited in museums and at fairs. Wealthy ladies wore aluminum spangles at their throats and wrists.

Aluminum was costly because sodium was rare and expensive. The cost of sodium made the cost of producing aluminum too great to allow commercial use of the latter.

Hamilton Y. Castner

It was quite reasonable to believe that the problem of producing cheaper aluminum could be solved by producing cheaper sodium. This idea appealed to a clever Brooklyn boy who was studying chemistry at Columbia University under Professor Chandler.

Hamilton Y. Castner was his name. A bronze tablet in his honor hangs at the entrance of Havemeyer Hall, Columbia University. Castner, while still a student, originated a new process for making sodium which brought the cost of that metal from several dollars a pound down to twenty cents. He put his process to work in the plant of Aluminum Company, Ltd., in Oldbury, England. By 1889 a production of 500 pounds of aluminum per day was reached. The production of aluminum was now on a commercial basis.

Charles Martin Hall

Unfortunately for Castner, another young man, Charles Martin Hall, while a student at Oberlin College, Oberlin, Ohio, became interested in aluminum and began experimenting to find a better way of producing it. He continued his work after graduation and in 1886 developed an electrolytic process for making aluminum which quickly snuffed the life out of the Deville-Castner sodium process. Although Castner's discovery was made too late to bring him any reward from the production of commercial aluminum through low-cost sodium, he earned fame later through other important discoveries in the field of chemistry.

Hall was only twenty-two years of age when he succeeded in accomplishing something that had baffled older and more learned chemists. Many savants had tried to extract aluminum from its ores with the aid of electricity. Before this could be accomplished, the aluminum ore had to be put in solution, that is, dissolved. Most aluminum compounds found in nature are difficult to dissolve. However, there are some strong chemicals that will dissolve alumina (aluminum oxide). These are water solutions and they cannot be used, because the water, instead of the alumina, breaks down when an electric current is passed through it.

Many important discoveries in science have been made by young men working with crude and meager facil-

CHARLES MARTIN HALL

COURTESY ALUMINUM COMPANY OF AMERICA

The twenty-two-year-old American chemist who discovered a secret which had eluded the world's scientists for decades, namely, the low-cost electrolytic process for separating aluminum from its ore.

COURTESY ALUMINUM COMPANY OF AMERICA

The woodshed laboratory where Charles Martin Hall devised the Hall electrochemical process for separating aluminum from its ores.

ities. A small crucible, a galvanic battery to supply electric current, and a burner installed in a woodshed laboratory constituted the equipment Charles Hall employed in his attempt to obtain aluminum with the aid of an electric current.

He sought a suitable solvent for aluminum ores. He puttered with this and that compound. Then came a day when he melted some CRYOLITE in his crucible. Cryolite is a snow-white, translucent, sodium-aluminum-fluoride mineral compound found only in Greenland. Hall added some aluminum ore in the form of ALUMINA to the molten cryolite. Alumina is known as emery in its crystalline form and is used as an abrasive for grinding. Rubies and sapphires are almost entirely alumina. The colors of these gems are due to minute quantities of impurities.

The alumina which Hall put into his crucible DIS-SOLVED IN THE MOLTEN CRYOLITE. His first attempt to send an electric current through the hot solution resulted in no metallic aluminum. He substituted a carbon crucible for the clay one he had been using. We can imagine his ecstasy when he found globules of molten aluminum in the carbon crucible. On February 23, 1886, Hall proudly showed his sisters a button of aluminum which had been produced by electric current. At last a way of making the electrons perform their magic with alumina had been found. A very young man had made a discovery which had baffled chemists for years. When an electric current from Hall's battery was passed through a molten mixture of alumina and cryolite, METALLIC ALU-MINUM COLLECTED AT THE NEGATIVE ELECTRODE. Hall applied for a patent on his process, and it was granted in 1889.

In 1886 the second interesting coincidence in aluminum research occurred. Paul L. T. Héroult, a young Frenchman, discovered the same process independently and simultaneously in France. Neither Hall nor Héroult knew of the other's work until Héroult applied for a patent in the United States. Hall, as already mentioned, obtained a United States patent. Héroult secured patent rights in France and in some other European countries.

Here in America the process used in the production of aluminum is known as the Hall Process, but in Europe it is known as the Héroult Process.

The discovery that metallic aluminum could be produced by dissolving alumina in molten cryolite and passing an electric current through the solution did not make aluminum available immediately in commercial quantities. There was more work to be done. For a few months, a group of Boston capitalists supplied Hall with money to carry on his experiments. But they soon lost faith in the possible commercial value of the research which their young chemist was conducting. Hall could not continue his experiments without financial assistance, so he sought help in the most logical place to find aid for an electrical smelting process. He went to Lockport, New York, where Alfred and Eugene Cowles had a plant equipped with what was at that time the largest dynamo in the world. Hall made an arrangement with the Cowles brothers which gave him an opportunity to try out his ideas on a large scale. Both Alfred and Eugene Cowles were skilled electrochemists. They had already succeeded in producing commercial quantities of aluminum alloyed with copper.

Hall remained with the Cowles brothers for a time; then he left and went to Pittsburgh, Pennsylvania. There he found an enterprising firm which had been formed by Alfred E. Hunt and George E. Clapp and was called the Pittsburgh Testing Laboratories. Hunt and Clapp furnished Hall with $20,000 for an experimental aluminum plant. In a short time Hall was turning out 50 pounds of aluminum per day. Here was actually more aluminum than the whole world wanted at that time. At first the metal was offered at $5 per pound. However, it accumulated so rapidly that the price was cut to $2 per pound in 1,000-pound lots.

Before there could be a large market for aluminum, it would be necessary to advertise it to acquaint consumers with the advantages of using the light-weight, silvery metal in place of iron, brass, and copper. More money was needed for promotion and marketing. Additional funds were obtained from two Pittsburgh bankers, Andrew W. Mellon and his brother Richard. A million-dollar corporation, called the Pittsburgh Reduction Company, was formed. Later the Pittsburgh Reduction Company changed its name to the Aluminum Company of America. The Aluminum Company of America is one of the largest and most profitable corporations in America. Charles Martin Hall became a very wealthy man. He died in Florida in 1914, leaving a large estate to be devoted to furthering education, one-third of it going to his alma mater, Oberlin College.

How Aluminum Is Produced Today

Strangely enough, clay, the most abundant compound of aluminum, is not the ore from which the metal is extracted commercially. Modern aluminum production is divided into two processes—the Bayer Process and the Hall Process. The Bayer Process produces ALUMINA from bauxite ore. Alumina is an impure aluminum oxide. The name "bauxite" comes from Baux, France, where it was first discovered.

A sketch of the Pittsburgh Reduction Company (since 1907, the Aluminum Company of America), in which aluminum production using the Hall process first began in 1888.

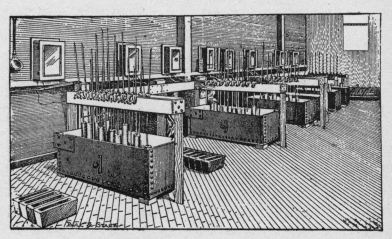

REDUCING POTS—PITTSBURGH REDUCTION COMPANY'S PROCESS.

The electrolytic cells, or "pots," used in the Pittsburgh Reduction Company's process for reducing alumina.

The Bayer Process involves a series of chemical treatments to separate the alumina from other elements in the ore. The ore is first crushed, then ground into small particles while immersed in a solution of caustic soda. The caustic soda dissolves only the aluminum content, leaving all other components behind as red mud. After the red mud is filtered out, the liquid (with the aluminum dissolved in it) is treated, to change it to aluminum hydroxide. Heating the aluminum hydroxide in huge kilns at 1,900 degrees F changes it into alumina, a powdery material resembling coarse granulated sugar in appearance.

From this pure alumina, which is a combination of aluminum with oxygen, metallic aluminum is obtained. The Hall electrolytic reduction process breaks up the union between aluminum and oxygen.

The electrolytic cells holding the molten cryolite and alumina in a modern aluminum smelter are steel tanks lined with carbon to form a cavity about 13 × 6 × 1 feet on the inside. The carbon lining protects the steel tank from the hot cryolite and acts as the cathode, or negative electrode. Alumina added to the molten cryolite * is the ELECTROLYTE. The cryolite is the SOLVENT. These terms are explained later in this book (refer to index). Large carbon blocks suspended above the cells and with their lower ends immersed in the molten contents form the anodes, or positive electrodes. A heavy electric current is passed through the solution between these two sets of electrodes. The current breaks down the alumina into

* Artificial cryolite instead of natural cryolite imported from Greenland.

aluminum and oxygen. The molten aluminum collects at the bottom of the cell and is drawn off every few days when a sufficient amount has accumulated. The oxygen combines with the carbon anodes and passes off as carbon dioxide gas. The aluminum which collects in the bottom of the cell is molten because the tremendous electric current passing through the solution heats it to a temperature of 1,900 degrees F.

HALL ALUMINUM PROCESS

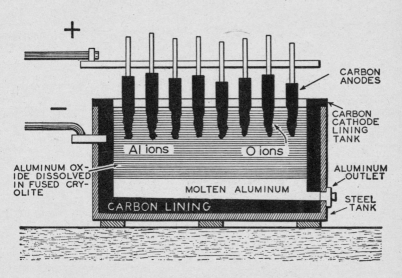

HOW ALUMINUM IS PRODUCED

The cells in which aluminum is obtained from alumina (aluminum oxide) by an electrochemical process are steel boxes lined with carbon. Carbon rods, arranged so that their lower ends dip into the cell, form the anodes, or positive electrodes. The carbon lining of the steel "pot" acts as the cathode, or negative electrode. Molten aluminum gathers on the bottom of the cell and is drawn off from time to time.

Theoretically, only about 2 volts is required to operate the cells, but 5 to 6 volts is used. The amperage is very large: in practice it varies between 8,000 and 50,000 amperes per cell. Each 1,000 amperes produces about 14 pounds of aluminum per day. The total amount of electric power consumed in an aluminum reduction plant to produce 1 pound of aluminum is nearly 12 kilowatt hours, or the same amount of energy that an ordinary electric flatiron consumes when operated continuously for 24 hours. It required more than 18,000,-000,000 kilowatt hours of electricity to produce the 920,000 tons of aluminum made in 1943, a year when war demanded high production. So great is the amount of electric power used in producing aluminum that most aluminum reduction plants are located near rivers where great power dams and electric generating facilities are available. Aluminum reduction plants are located at Niagara Falls, New York, Massena, New York, in the Tennessee Valley Authority area, and near Bonneville Dam on the Columbia River.

An Explanation of the Hall Aluminum Process in the Words of an Electrochemist

As described in the language of an electrochemist, here is what happens when aluminum is produced by the Hall Process:

The action of breaking down the alumina by an electric current is called ELECTROLYSIS, ELECTROLYTIC REDUCTION, and ELECTROLYZING. The aluminum oxide, dissolved in molten cryolite, dissociates and forms ions, just as any electrolyte does when it is dissolved in water. The ions formed are those of aluminum and oxygen. The aluminum ions carry positive charges of electricity, and the oxygen ions carry negative charges of electricity. The passage of a direct current through the molten alumina-cryolite from one electrode to the other attracts the positive aluminum ions to the cathode and produces metallic aluminum, which falls to the bottom of the cell. The oxygen ions, since they carry a negative charge, are attracted to the carbon anodes. There they are relieved of their charge and liberated as free oxygen. Oxygen has a strong tendency to unite with carbon under the proper circumstances. One of the proper circumstances is the presence of heat. Since the molten contents of the cell have a temperature of 1,800 to 1,900 degrees F and the carbon rods are at least equally hot, there is a union of the oxygen with carbon to form first carbon monoxide and later carbon dioxide. Consequently, the carbon anodes are rapidly consumed and must be replaced frequently.

The process is a continuous one; molten aluminum is drawn off through an outlet at the bottom of the cell; more alumina and new carbon anodes are added at intervals.

SALT

A Common Chemical Which Is Grist for the Electrochemist

Among the treasures to which mankind has fallen heir from the great cornucopia of nature is an almost unlimited supply of little crystal cubes of sodium and chlorine—in plain every-day language, common table salt. These are found wherever sea water has evaporated. The accepted presence of the salt shaker on your dining table has obscured its real importance. Not only is salt a necessity for the health of the human body, it is also a chemical jewel box.

For long ages, salt was put to no other use than seasoning food, preserving fish and meat, and tanning leather. No one but a chemist would have thought of doing anything else with it. It was the chemist who made salt significant to each of us personally; thanks to him, the clothes and shoes we wear, the newspapers and books we read, the water we drink, and the soap we use are made better by the use of salt in their manufacture. Salt is used for preserving and curing hides and tanning leather. It is the only practical source of hydrochloric acid, a highly important chemical of commerce. Salt is a raw material for making such useful compounds as sodium carbonate, sodium bicarbonate, sodium sulfate, sodium hydroxide, and sodium hypochlorite.

Salt is obtained in two ways—by evaporation of brine and by mining of rock salt. There are two kinds of brine —surface brine, and brine from wells. Surface brine comes from sea water or salt lakes, while brine from wells is either natural salt water or is made by pumping water into wells drilled into underground deposits of rock salt.

What Is Salt?

Pure salt is one of the simpler chemical compounds. Its chemical name is SODIUM CHLORIDE. It consists of an atom of sodium combined with an atom of chlorine. It seems almost unbelievable that a soft, silvery, poisonous metal and an irritating, poisonous, green gas could join together and form harmless little cubes of white table salt, a necessity in the diet of men and animals. In brine the electrochemist has available the atoms of four elements—sodium, chlorine, oxygen, and hydrogen—with which to perform tricks.

Chemical Great-grandparents

Most of the chemical products that play an extremely important part in our daily lives, substances so essential that the very life and health of entire communities depend upon them, have never been seen and are scarcely known even by name to the average person. The two substances which the electrochemist has conjured out of common salt with the aid of electricity are among them. Sodium hydroxide and chlorine are their names; and these two substances are the great-grandparents of hundreds of useful chemicals. A whole library of books could be written about manufacturing operations which require sodium hydroxide or chlorine. Just as pine and oak furnish lumber from which innumerable objects can be made, so these two chemicals furnish a chemical lumber for great industries.

SODIUM HYDROXIDE

Sodium hydroxide is a white, waxy-looking solid which dissolves easily in water. It is commonly called caustic soda. When concentrated, sodium hydroxide is highly corrosive, destroying the skin and attacking a great many substances. It dissolves animal fibers, like wool, silk, and hair. Large amounts are used by the rubber, petroleum, paper, rayon, explosive, dye, drug, and general chemical industries.

When sodium hydroxide is allowed to act upon cotton cloth under proper control, the cotton fibers undergo a change and acquire considerable luster. This is the process called mercerizing. Practically all of the soap manufactured at the present time is made by treating fats and oils with caustic soda. A by-product of soap-making is GLYCEROL, commonly known as glycerin. From glycerin comes DYNAMITE. These are only a few of the modern uses of sodium hydroxide.

CHLORINE—A GERM-KILLER

Chlorine is a greenish-yellow gas which derived its name from a Greek word meaning "pale green." Chlorine was first isolated by the Swedish chemist Scheele in 1774. In 1810, Humphry Davy proved chlorine to be an element.

Chlorine plays an important part in our present-day complex civilization. Over 10,000,000 tons is used annually in the United States. Chlorine has powerful sterilizing properties. It is also a bleach. Either alone or as a constituent of bleaching powder it will whiten cotton. In the form of bleaching powder, chlorine played an important part in the development of the British textile industry. Bleaching is an essential part of manufacturing cotton textiles. At one time, it was accomplished by laying the cloth on the grass in the sun. If sunlight were used as a bleach now, the enormous output of modern cotton mills would require several counties as bleaching fields. Using chlorine, manufacturers can bleach thousands of yards of cloth quickly in a small tank.

Chlorine will kill typhoid and other disease germs in water. In one form or another, we find chlorine used in the textile and paper industries, in reservoirs and swimming pools, in hospitals, laundries, dairies, food factories, and farms. It is used in making coal-tar dyes, chloroform, carbon tetrachloride fire-extinguisher and cleaning fluid, benzoate of soda, and hydrochloric acid, and for purifying oils and making valuable medicines.

A generation ago, many parts of the world were veritable hotbeds of typhoid fever because of pollution of the drinking water. Then came the discovery that less than one drop of liquid chlorine in 50 gallons of water will kill all the bacteria present. A thousand times this amount of chlorine in water would still be harmless to human beings, but more is unnecessary. Soon hospitals started to become free of typhoid cases. Nowadays typhoid is seldom heard of. Three-fourths of all the water in the United States supplied for household purposes is chlorine-treated. We can turn on a faucet and fill our glasses with clear, germ-free drinking water, thanks to the protecting action of chlorine.

The Electrolytic Method of Producing Sodium Hydroxide and Chlorine

About one-half the total amount of sodium hydroxide used in this country, and all of the chlorine, is made by the electrolysis of common salt. The electrochemist is primarily interested in the production of chlorine. The caustic soda and hydrogen which are produced simultaneously are by-products, or accessory products. There are several large chlorine-producing plants at Niagara Falls. Large underground salt deposits that occupy the beds of prehistoric salt lakes in western New York supply the salt. The falling water of the Niagara River supplies the electric power.

A visit to a chlorine plant reveals row upon row of cylindrical tanks (called cells) connected to pipes and bus-bars (main conductors). The pipes carry away the chlorine and hydrogen, the bus-bars feed current to the cells. The hydrogen is dried, compressed, and stored in steel cylinders. It is used for welding and in many chemical manufacturing processes. The chlorine gas is dried, compressed, and liquified. It reaches the market in strong steel cylinders.

All the cells employ graphite as anodes, because it is one of the few materials which resist the chemical action of chlorine. The cathodes, or negative electrodes, of the cells are steel.

Technical Explanation of the Commercial Process
Used to Produce Chlorine by Electrolysis

Two somewhat similar types of electrolytic cells have been developed for producing chlorine commercially by the electrolysis of sodium chloride. One is called the Nelson Cell; the other is the Vorce Cell. They employ the same principles but differ slightly in mechanical design. Each cell consists of two steel tanks, one within the other. The inner tank in both types of cell has a perforated wall.

About 1.7 kilowatt-hours of electrical energy is required to produce 1 pound of chlorine. This means that the total chlorine produced daily in the United States requires a daily consumption of over 20 billion kilowatt-hours of electrical energy.

When an electric current flows through the brine in both types of cell, chlorine collects at the anode, and sodium hydroxide and hydrogen at the cathode.

If the chlorine and sodium hydroxide come into contact with each other, they react to form sodium hypochlorite (NaOCl) and other products. To prevent this, both the Nelson and Vorce Cells are designed so that the anode is separated from the cathode by a porous diaphragm. The cathode is the inner, perforated steel tank and is lined with a thick layer of asbestos. When this tank is filled with brine, the brine seeps through the asbestos lining until it makes contact with the perforated steel cathode. A row of graphite anodes dips into the brine in the cathode tank. When the current is turned on, chlorine is liberated on the surfaces of the graphite anodes. It bubbles up through the brine and is led off through a pipe connected to the top of the cell. Hydrogen is liberated on the surface of the perforated steel cathode but is prevented from mixing with the chlorine by the asbestos diaphragm. The hydrogen is led out from the space between the two tanks through a pipe at the top of the cell. Sodium hydroxide is formed in the brine

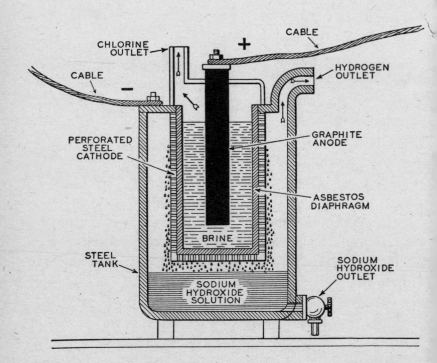

NELSON CELL FOR DECOMPOSING SALT BY ELECTRIC CURRENT

The electric current passes through a strong brine solution (salt dissolved in water) contained in a perforated steel cylinder lined with porous asbestos. The products are caustic soda (sodium hydroxide), chlorine, and hydrogen.

where it soaks through the asbestos and makes contact with the perforated steel anode. As more brine soaks through the asbestos, it carries with it the sodium hydroxide and drips into the compartment between the two tanks, from which it is continuously removed. Fresh brine is added to the inner compartment in order to maintain the supply.

The mixture of brine and sodium hydroxide that is removed from the cell contains about 8 per cent sodium hydroxide and 15 per cent unchanged sodium chloride. The sodium hydroxide and sodium chloride are separated by filtration and evaporation.

To understand fully the electrolytic process which occurs in the Nelson and Vorce Cells, it is necessary to consider the ions which form in a brine solution. Water ionizes to a minute degree, and consequently there are H^+ and OH^- ions present. Sodium chloride yields Na^+ and Cl^- ions. The Cl^- ions are discharged almost immediately at the anode and escape from the solution as chlorine gas. The electrons lost by the chlorine ions are taken up by the hydrogen ions at the cathode, and the hydrogen ions become hydrogen molecules. This leaves OH^- ions and Na^+ ions in the solution. Upon evaporation of water from the mother liquor, the Na^+ and OH^- ions combine and form solid sodium hydroxide ($NaOH$).

SODIUM: A Soft, Waxy Metal Produced from Salt

The electrochemist's legerdemain with salt is not confined to sending an electric current through a water solution of salt. By passing a current through molten and purified sodium chloride, he produces chlorine and metallic sodium.

Sodium is a strange metal. It has characteristics which we do not usually associate with a metallic substance. It is soft and waxlike at ordinary temperatures; in fact, it is easily cut with a knife. It melts at a temperature slightly below the boiling point of water. Sodium's silvery surface tarnishes quickly in air, and in the laboratory sodium is kept immersed in kerosene to prevent contact with air. Sodium has an aggressive personality and in the

METALLIC SODIUM

Sodium reacts violently with water. Science teachers sometimes demonstrate the reaction between sodium and water to their classes. Metallic sodium is too dangerous for boys and girls to handle. Sodium for experimental purposes in the laboratory is kept immersed in kerosene oil to protect it from moisture in the atmosphere.

SODIUM

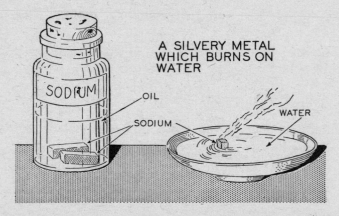

A SILVERY METAL WHICH BURNS ON WATER

OIL

SODIUM

SODIUM

WATER

laboratory is handled with a pair of tongs. It reacts strongly with water, forming hydrogen and sodium hydroxide.

$$2\ Na + 2\ H_2O \rightarrow H_2 + 2\ NaOH$$

A lump of sodium placed on water (it floats) reacts vigorously, rolling and zigzagging about on the surface, spluttering, and not infrequently catching fire, igniting the hydrogen, and leading, sometimes, to a small explosion. It is, therefore, not only useless but very dangerous to use water on a sodium fire.

One might well ask, "Why manufacture such an unstable metal?" Sodium has many uses in the laboratory and is useful to the manufacturing chemist as a raw material to combine with other elements. More than 250,000,000 pounds are produced every year in the United States to be used in the manufacture of tetraethyl lead, the "anti-knock" material in gasoline which is sold under the name "ethyl gas." It is produced by the reaction betwen ethyl chloride and a sodium lead alloy.

$$4\ C_2H_4Cl + Na_4Pb \rightarrow Pb(C_2H_5)_4 + 4\ NaCl$$

A vast tonnage also finds its way into the manufacture of dyestuffs, cyanides for electroplating and metal refining, plastics, and sodium peroxide. Sodium is an excellent conductor of heat, and it is sometimes used in machines to transfer heat where heat must be applied or removed quickly. For example, the stem, or shank, of the exhaust valve in an airplane engine is made hollow and filled with molten sodium. The sodium helps to conduct the heat from the hot valve heads. Every time an exhaust valve opens in an airplane engine, a blast of flame rushes past the valve head. The head must be kept as cool as possible if it is not soon to become pitted and warped. Sodium and oxygen have a strong affinity for each other. Consequently, sodium can be used to extract oxygen and other impurities from other metals. A small amount of an alloy of sodium and zinc or sodium and lead introduced into molten metals such as brass or bronze will abstract oxygen and other impurities and produce stronger, more uniform products.

Sodium is one of several metals which will emit electrons under the influence of light. This property is utilized in the construction of photoelectric cells, or "electric eyes." Metallic sodium and chlorine are produced simultaneously at Niagara Falls, New York, by a process invented by J. C. Downs. A vertical cross section of the Downs Cell is illustrated. The operation is based upon passing an electric current through fused sodium chloride. (See page 95.)

Sodium chloride as required is fed into the cell through an opening at the top. Upon the passage of direct current through the cell, chlorine is liberated at the carbon anode **A**. The gas rises through the fused salt, collects in the chamber above the anode, and passes out through a pipe. Sodium is liberated at the ring-shaped iron or copper cathode **C**. The molten sodium collects in the ring-shaped chamber **S**, rises through the pipe **P**, and overflows into the tank **T**. The chlorine and metallic sodium are both collected separately and away from contact with air. Any water in the sodium chloride crystals is driven out when the salt fuses and escapes into the air as vapor.

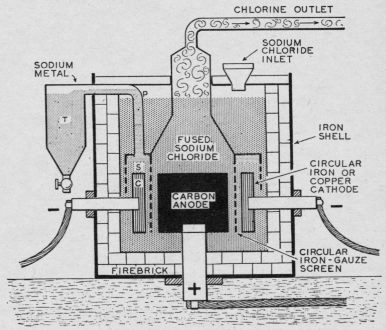

DOWNS CELL FOR PRODUCTION OF SODIUM BY THE ELECTROLYSIS OF FUSED SODIUM CHLORIDE
For explanation see text, page 94.

ELECTROCHEMISTRY
PRODUCES METALS AND ALLOYS

Impossible with wood- or coal- or oil-fired furnaces

Five and six thousand years ago the Chinese and Egyptians fabricated jewelry, statues, vases, weapons, and household necessities from metals. They were very limited in the choice of material for metalwork because there were only six known metals in that ancient world. These were gold, silver, copper, tin, lead, and mercury. Iron probably became known later (about 3,000 B.C.). Today the chemist, metallurgist, and artisan have at their command over SEVENTY metals and many thousands of alloys. The alloys vary in their characteristics as widely as the basic metals, and consequently there is an almost unlimited choice of metals to work with.

The electrolytic cell and the electric furnace provide the best, and only practical, method of producing many of our most useful metals and alloys.

Several of these processes are described briefly in the remainder of this chapter and in the chapter following.

MAGNESIUM: A Twentieth-Century Metal

From magnesium chloride, electrochemistry produces a twentieth-century metal, the light, silvery-white magnesium. It is one of the lightest metals, weighing only two-thirds as much as aluminum. A bar of magnesium 1 inch square and 64 inches long weighs only 4 pounds. A bar of the same size made of steel weighs 18¼ pounds, more than four times as much. Magnesium is easily tarnished by moist air. When heated in air, it ignites at a comparatively low temperature and burns brilliantly. Burning magnesium produces the brilliant white light of fireworks, flares, and star shells. The alloys of magnesium with aluminum, such as Magnalium, Duralumin, Alloy 17S, Aladur, Aldrey and Almelec, possess lightness and great strength. Duralumin, a heat-treated alloy of aluminum with magnesium, copper, and manganese, was the first of the light-weight, strong alloys which provide structural material for building modern airplanes.

It is said that the element magnesium derives its name from Magnesia, a town in Asia Minor. For a long time the United States was forced to buy all the metallic magnesium it consumed from Germany. No one outside of Germany knew how to produce the metal economically. But after several American chemists experimented for several years, the secret of magnesium manufacture was found and the process became well established in this country.

·

A SILVERY METAL WHOSE WEIGHT IS LESS THAN ONE QUARTER THAT OF STEEL

Among the impurities in common salt is magnesium chloride. Sending an electric current through fused magnesium chloride produces pure magnesium, a useful metal which weighs only two-thirds as much as aluminum. The illustration shows the comparative sizes of equal weights of magnesium and steel. Duralumin, Magnalium, Aladur, and Almelec are strong, light-weight alloys of magnesium and aluminum.

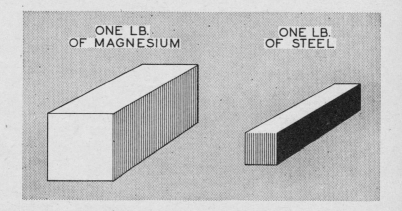

ONE LB.
OF MAGNESIUM

ONE LB.
OF STEEL

Although magnesium occurs in great abundance in combination with other minerals, these compounds cannot be used as a source of metallic magnesium. The metal is produced by passing a direct current through fused magnesium chloride. At present, sea water and Michigan salt brines are the important sources of magnesium chloride in the United States. The natural brine pumped from deep wells in Michigan contains about 3 per cent magnesium chloride ($MgCl_2$). The process takes place in large rectangular steel pots which hold several tons of melted magnesium chloride. A furnace is provided under each pot to melt the magnesium chloride and maintain the proper working temperature. Metallic magnesium is liberated at graphite anodes immersed in the molten chloride. The steel pot serves as the cathode. Being lighter than the molten chloride from which it is electrolyzed, the melted metallic magnesium rises to the top and flows off into a collecting chamber. Thus, from an impurity found in small quantities in table salt the interesting, useful metal magnesium is secured.

CERIUM, CALCIUM, LITHIUM, BERYLLIUM—

More Metals of the Modern Age

CERIUM. By sending a direct current through fused cerium chloride, the electrochemist secures metallic cerium. An alloy of cerium and iron is pyrophoric, that is, it gives off sparks when rubbed against a rough iron surface. It is this alloy which forms the so-called "flints" used in cigarette lighters.

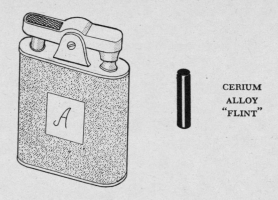

CERIUM
ALLOY
"FLINT"

CERIUM—ONE OF THE METALS OF THE MODERN AGE PRODUCED BY ELECTROCHEMISTRY

The so-called "flints" in cigarette lighters are an alloy of cerium and iron.

CALCIUM. Calcium is a silver-white crystalline metal somewhat harder than lead. It reacts with cold water and, like magnesium, burns with a brilliant flame in air. Compounds of calcium are widely distributed in the form of limestone, gypsum, alabaster, marble, chalk, coral, and sea shells. Plants and animals require considerable amounts of calcium. Calcium phosphate is the principal component of bones and teeth.

Sir Humphry Davy first isolated metallic calcium in 1808 by passing a current of electricity through calcium hydroxide. Today the metal is secured by passing a direct current through a fused bath of calcium chloride to which a small amount of calcium fluoride is usually added to lower the melting point. The graphite crucible which contains the fused chlorides is the anode. The cathode is an iron rod, suspended in the molten chlorides, and is movable. It can be raised or lowered as necessary. As the molten metallic calcium appears, it rises to the iron cathode and solidifies on it. The cathode is slowly raised as the calcium is deposited. This produces an irregular-shaped stick of metallic calcium called a "cabbage stalk."

What is metallic calcium used for? Many things. Some petroleum refineries use it to remove sulfur from lubricating oils. An alloy of lead and calcium is used in bearings and as a sheath for telephone cables. Calcium has such an affinity for oxygen that it is often used to reduce the oxides of tungsten, chromium, uranium, and beryllium to the metal. An alloy of calcium and silicon is employed as a deoxidizer in melting steel, copper, and some other metals.

LITHIUM.   Lithium is the lightest of all metals. Like sodium, magnesium, and calcium, the metal is secured by the electrolysis of its fused chloride. Lithium is of no use as a metal except when alloyed with other metals. The addition of a very small amount of lithium improves iron and copper used for castings. It is used in small quantities in bearing metals such as Bahnmetal, an alloy of calcium, lithium, sodium, and lead produced in Germany for railroad cars.

BERYLLIUM.   Here is a metal which is 30 per cent lighter than aluminum but much harder. At present, the only commercial source of beryllium is the mineral beryl, a beryllium-aluminum silicate that, theoretically, can contain 14 per cent beryllium oxide. Metallic beryllium can be produced by both chemical and electrochemical processes.

In the United States the commercial production of beryllium did not begin until 1939. Its applications have multiplied ever since, and we may expect greatly increased use of this metal in the future. An alloy consisting of 30 per cent aluminum and 70 per cent beryllium is lighter than aluminum and has greater tensile strength than Duralumin. It is used in aircraft construction. An alloy of nickel and beryllium makes excellent high-speed bearings suitable for aircraft engines. An alloy of beryllium, nickel, cobalt, chromium, and molybdenum is used to make surgical and dental instruments. The addition of 2.5 per cent beryllium to copper produces an alloy which after heat treatment is six times as strong as pure copper and an excellent material for springs. Beryllium-copper springs have great resistance to corrosion and to the "fatigue" that causes ordinary springs to break.

One of the uses of beryllium is particularly interesting: pressed into small plates 1 to 2 millimeters thick, it is used as windows in x-ray tubes. It permits 17 times as much radiation to pass as any other material which can be used. Beryllium has numerous uses in the atomic energy field as a reflector and as a moderator to slow down neutrons in the atomic reactor or atomic pile.

PURIFYING METALS
BY MEANS OF ELECTROLYSIS

Many metals are purified by the electrochemical process called ELECTROLYTIC REFINING. The list includes copper, nickel, lead, silver, tin, gold, bismuth, and, on a small scale, many other metals not so well known.

The principle of electrolytic refining is always the same, no matter which metal is purified by its magic. An electric current does the trick; it causes the impure metal to dissolve in a liquid electrolyte and then to reappear in PURE metallic form. The impurities are left behind in the electrolyte in the form of sludge, or "mud."

COPPER—THE RED METAL

Next to iron, copper is the most useful metal. One of the great milestones of cultural progress was the discovery and use of copper. Mankind then left the Stone Age and entered the Bronze Age. Copper belongs to the same chemical family as silver and gold. Because it is often found free in nature like the other members of its family, man was able to use it without smelting or roasting its ores. With this native metal and its natural alloys (bronze is a copper alloy which contains tin and may have zinc and lead added) ancient man was able to make tools and other articles of a usefulness and intricacy impossible with stone. The Latin name for copper, *cuprum*, comes from Cyprus, the Mediterranean island where ancient copper mines, long since worked out, once existed. The world utilizes an enormous amount of copper. Copper has the highest electrical conductivity of any of the non-precious metals. Consequently, almost all electrical wires and conductors (a small percentage are aluminum) are copper.

Inventions and discoveries constantly bring new demands for this soft, red metal. The electromagnetic windings on motors and generators are wound with copper wire. There are tiny electromagnets wound with pure copper wire in the receiver of your telephone. The world's telephone and telegraph messages travel from place to place over copper wires. Electrical power is distributed over the countryside through networks of copper wires and cables. Aluminum cables reinforced with steel are also used for power distribution but not nearly to the extent to which copper is used.

All coins contain copper. The ordinary American one-cent piece is made of a bronze which is 95 per cent copper, 4 per cent tin, and 1 per cent zinc. Nickels and quarters have a copper core covered by layers of cupronickel. Gold and silver coins are hardened and made more resistant to wear by the addition of 10 per cent copper.

Copper Alloys

The properties of copper are greatly changed when it is alloyed with different metals. Thus, copper may be made more easily machinable, and hardened and toughened. There are many copper alloys, any one of which may be varied greatly. The following are common copper alloys:

Brass is copper alloyed with 18 to 45 per cent of zinc. Stronger, it is more easily machined than pure copper.

The name "bronze" was originally applied to an alloy consisting chiefly of copper and tin. Now there are many bronzes.

Phosphor bronze is an alloy of copper, tin, and phosphorus. It is used to make small springs.

Manganese bronze is an alloy of copper, zinc, aluminum, iron, and manganese. It is resistant to salt water and is used for rudders, boat shafts, propellers, and marine fittings.

Aluminum bronze is a white alloy of copper, aluminum (10 to 15 per cent), and a small amount of iron and is used in architectural and ornamental work.

Silicon bronze is copper to which small amounts of silicon and manganese have been added. It is chemically resistant and has much greater tensile strength than pure copper.

Gun metal is a copper alloy containing about 10 per cent of tin and 2 per cent of zinc.

Nickel silver is a silver-white alloy of copper, zinc, and nickel.

Most metals are of a silvery color, but copper has a reddish luster. Its true appearance is usually masked by a surface coating that copper, because of its chemical activity, readily acquires by interaction with substances in the atmosphere. This surface coating, or film, as a chemist would prefer to call it, may be copper oxide, copper sulfide, copper carbonate, or a mixture of these compounds. When an electrician scrapes wires before splicing them, he is removing the surface film. The film does not conduct electricity so well as copper—it impedes the flow of current and so must be removed from splices and joints. To see the real rosy luster of copper, you must clean and polish it.

Copper does not change in dry air, but in moist air it becomes covered gradually with a green layer of copper carbonate. The light green coating that copper roofs, gutters, coins, statues, and other objects acquire on exposure to the weather is a complex variety of copper carbonate. Once formed, it constitutes a resistant layer that protects the metal beneath more effectively than any paint could. The green coating on weathered copper is not VERDIGRIS, as it is often erroneously called. True verdigris is COPPER ACETATE, formed by the action of acetic acid upon copper. It can be made as an experiment by leaving a strip of copper immersed in vinegar for several days.

The ability of copper to conduct an electric current, its tensile strength, and its ductility, or stretching and bending qualities, are seriously impaired by small amounts of impurities dissolved in the metal. To be most satisfactory for electrical and some mechanical work, copper must be practically 100 per cent pure. Electrolytic refining produces pure copper at lower cost than any other method. A description of the process of refining copper by the electrolytic method will explain the use of electrolysis in winning metals away from their impurities.

Electrolytic Copper Refining

The extraction of copper from its ores does not produce pure copper immediately. It results in crude copper containing cuprous oxide, cuprous sulfide, the precious metals gold, silver, and platinum, and other metals such as antimony, arsenic, tellurium, and selenium. The simplest and also the cheapest way of refining crude copper is an electrochemical process. Hence a large proportion of the copper which reaches the market is purified at the refinery by electrolysis. This method produces copper in which the amount of impurities remaining in the copper is so small that their presence can be shown only by the most refined tests.

A copper refinery serves a twofold purpose. Not only does it produce the high-grade copper required in commerce and especially in the electrical industry, but it recovers the precious metals which crude copper contains. It is estimated that three-quarters of all the silver and about one-quarter of all the gold produced in the world are obtained in refining copper, lead, nickel, and cobalt. The copper refinery is actually a more important silver producer than the silver mines.

The United States refines most of the world's copper. Crude copper in the form of "blister"; copper cake; and the dust called "cement" copper come to American refineries from Arizona, Utah, Montana, Canada, Chile, and the faraway Katanga Mines in Africa. Refineries are located on the seacoast, whence the copper can be shipped to all parts of the world and inland to points of copper consumption.

At the refinery, the crude copper is dumped into large furnaces in which it is melted. The molten copper is then poured into molds to form large rectangular slabs with ears, or lugs, at the upper corners. These are the ANODES. They are still crude copper. When they have cooled, they are ready for refining.

A number of anodes are hung in a tank about 12 feet long, between 3 and 4 feet wide, and about 3 or 4 feet deep. There are rows and rows of these tanks in a refinery. One lug, or ear, of each anode rests on a copper bus-bar at the side of the tank. A bus-bar is one of the main bars, or conductors, carrying an electric current. Between each pair of anodes is hung a thin sheet of pure copper also connected to a bus-bar. These sheets are the CATHODES, or starting sheets, upon which the refined copper will be deposited as soon as the tank is put into operation. All anodes are, as the electrical engineer would say, IN PARALLEL, and the cathodes are similarly connected. The tanks are filled with a solution of copper sulfate and sulfuric acid. In this instance, "parallel" means that all the anodes are connected together to a positive bus-bar and all cathodes are connected together to a negative bus-bar.

The bus-bars carry direct current from a large generator to the tanks. The current travels through the copper sulfate-sulfuric acid solution from the anodes to the cathodes. The electric current in its passage from the anode into the solution causes some of the crude copper to dissolve and go into solution. The copper ions (electrically charged atoms of copper) thus formed move through the solution to the cathode and are deposited there as metallic copper. The once thin starting sheets soon grow into thick copper slabs 99.94 to 99.97 per cent pure. They are lifted out of the tanks by an over-head crane, carried away, washed, and dried, in preparation for the cathode, or "wire bar," furnace. Here they are melted and poured into molds which form wire bars, ingots, billets, slabs, cakes, and the various special shapes of refined copper best suited to the copper rolling mill, wire drawing mill, tube mill, foundry, etc., where the copper is to be fabricated into finished form.

Valuable Mud

During the electrolytic copper refining process, the precious metals and impurities in the crude copper anodes, such as gold, silver, antimony, lead, and arsenic do not dissolve in the copper sulfate and sulfuric acid solution. They fall to the bottom of the tank as "mud" or adhere to the anodes as slime. The "anode mud," as it is called at the refinery, is collected from the bottom of the tanks and filtered. No one but a chemist would ever suspect that this slippery muck is literally worth its weight in gold. When the moisture has drained off, the filtered mud forms a cake which is roasted, treated with sulfuric acid, washed, and again filtered. The slimy substance which is left is then melted once more and refined in a small "doré" furnace. During this part of the process, the lead and related materials form a slag which is skimmed off. Later, lead is recovered from this slag.

It is said that the Chicago meat packers have found out how to utilize every part of an animal except its squeal when it is slaughtered. The copper refineries carry their process to almost the same degree of efficiency. Any antimony present in the mud volatilizes and is collected with the dust from the flues and chimneys connected to the furnaces. The addition of soda ash to the molten slime in the furnace forms a slag containing selenium and tellurium which is skimmed off. Selenium is used in the electrical and electronics industry to make photo-electric cells and rectifiers. Tellurium is used in lead alloys to increase their strength and acid resistance. When most of the contaminating metals have been re-covered, there are left only gold, silver, and small quan-tities of platinum and palladium in a combination known as DORÉ metal. Molten doré metal is cast into anodes for use in Thum Electrolytic Cells which separate the silver from other metals.

Gold and Silver Recovered by Electrochemical Methods

Men have known of silver about as long as they have known of gold. Silver was used as a medium of barter centuries ago. The first metal coined as money in Greece and Rome was silver. Because of its beauty and also because of the ease with which it is worked, silver has long been in favor for coins and jewelry. It is widely used in the manufacture of tableware. So-called "solid" silver contains a small percentage of copper to increase its hardness. Enormous quantities of silver compounds, particularly silver bromide, are used in photography.

The Thum Cells used to recover silver as a by-product from copper refining are shallow porcelain boxes con-taining a wooden basket lined with duck or linen. The basket holds the electrodes in a horizontal position and retains the anode mud or slime which forms as the metallic silver crystals, 99.99 per cent pure, are being deposited on the cathode by the electric current.

Even after the silver is recovered, the refining process is still not complete. The slime remaining in the cloth bag or on the linen diaphragm of the wooden basket still contains gold, platinum, and palladium. Gold is worth much more than the same weight of copper. Platinum is even more valuable. After being washed with sulfuric acid, the slime is melted and cast into anodes for use in the gold-refining cells. Thin gold cathodes, corresponding to the starting sheets used in the copper-refining cells, collect pure gold deposited out of the electrolyte from the anode by the passage of the electric current. Platinum and palladium remain in the electrolyte and are recovered by chemical methods rather than by electrochemical means.

Platinum and the Platinum-Group Metals

Platinum is a dense white metal which looks like silver and tin but is a precious metal. It costs more than gold. During World War II platinum was stabilized at a ceiling price of $35 per ounce, but since then the price has soared as high as $189 per ounce.

Although a large percentage of the world's platinum production goes into jewelry, the bulk of platinum and platinum-group metals is used in the electrical and chemical industries and in dentistry and medicine.

The platinum-group metals include platinum, palladium, iridium, osmium, rhodium, and ruthenium. Platinum is the most plentiful and most widely used member of the group, but the others are increasing in importance.

The platinum-group metals have numerous electrical applications. Platinum and platinum alloys are employed in many delicate electrical and laboratory instruments, in electronic tubes, voltage regulators, relays, high-tension magnetos. Palladium is used widely in the contacts of telephone relays. Ruthenium and osmium are employed in many hard alloys for the tips of fountain pens and phonograph needles.

Chemical laboratories use platinum utensils and equipment. Pure platinum and platinum-iridium alloys are used as insoluble anodes in various electroplating processes. Platinum-gold and platinum-rhodium alloys are used to make spinnerettes (nozzles with tiny holes) for making rayon fibers from viscose. Fiber glass is produced by forcing molten glass through tiny platinum nozzles. Platinum in spongy or colloidal form is used as a catalyst in the synthesis of sulfuric acid and the oxidation of ammonia to nitric acid. As a catalytic agent or catalyst, the platinum does not enter into the reactions. It merely brings about and speeds the reactions. It can be used over and over again. Platinized asbestos and colloidal platinum are also active catalysts.

Platinum and palladium alloys are used extensively in dentistry for anchorages, pins, and dentures.

Platinum is never found in nature as a pure metal but is always associated with gold, copper, nickel, iron, chromite, and the metals of the platinum-group. Crude placer platinum is recovered by methods essentially similar to those used for recovering placer gold, except that none of the platinum-group metals respond to amalgamation (mixing with mercury), a process common in placer gold recovery. A placer metal is obtained from the earth by washing an alluvial or glacial deposit containing particles of metal.

Russia leads in the world production of platinum and the platinum-group metals, followed by South Africa, Canada, the U.S.A. and Colombia.

The platinum and platinum-group metals recovered by Canadian refineries are by-products of the electrolytic refining of nickel and copper. In many instances the detailed procedures used by the various refineries are closely guarded trade secrets. It is known, however, that the platinum-group residues from the refining of nickel, copper, and gold are recovered by a combination of complex smelting, chemical, and electrolytic processes.

Chapter Seven

Products of the Electric Furnace

The electric furnace is an important contribution of science and engineering to the economic, social, and intellectual life of mankind. Without electric furnaces to produce abrasives and alloy steels, automobiles would be too expensive for any but the rich. A complete list of electric furnace products and their uses would be tiresome.

Electrolytic processes are interesting and important, but a plant where they are carried out is not a bit theatrical. The cells are quiet; the spectator sees little activity. On the other hand, electric furnace operations are usually spectacular. Sizzling, dazzling infernos, white-hot liquid metals poured into crucibles and molds, the faint hum of vast energy rushing through huge electrodes are to be seen or heard.

OUR MOST USEFUL METAL

Among the more than seventy metallic elements are some that are hard, some that are soft, some that are scarce, and some that are plentiful. With such a wide choice at the disposal of the chemist, metallurgist, and artisan, there is nevertheless one metal which is more plentiful, costs less, and has more valuable mechanical properties than any of the others. It is iron—our most useful metal. The one metal which forms the basis of our modern civilization is iron. Almost every type of industrial activity in our age of machinery is dependent, in one way or another, on iron, and on the steel which is made from iron.

The supply of copper, tin, lead, and zinc is alarmingly limited in comparison with that of iron. Iron is provided by nature in some measure in all rocks and earths. There are vast beds of useful iron ore on the earth's surface which are still unmined. Except for iron meteorites hurtled to our earth from outer space, iron is never found in a natural state, as are gold, silver, and copper. It is always in combination with some other element. It is separated from its ores by smelting in a blast furnace and is made into crude castings called PIGS. The cost of converting high-grade iron ore into pig iron is relatively small. The number of tons of pig iron produced by the blast furnaces in operation is one of the indications of this country's prosperity. Cast iron and the various steels are made from pig iron. Cast iron is a commercial variety of iron containing more than 1.7 per cent carbon which can be poured molten into a sand mold so that it will solidify in a desired shape. It is brittle and not so strong as steel but is more easily fusible. Steel is produced by refining pig iron and is distinguished by its lower carbon content (any amount up to about 1.7 per cent). Mild, or soft, steel has roughly less than 0.25 per cent carbon; medium steel contains roughly 0.25 to 0.60 per cent carbon; and high carbon steel has roughly more than 0.60 per cent carbon. The alloy steels contain various amounts of silicon, manganese, vanadium, nickel, and chromium. They have great strength and are called manganese steel, vanadium steel, etc., according to the metal with which the iron is alloyed.

Because the mechanical properties of the various irons and steels are superior to those of other metals for some purposes, iron and steel build our automobiles, bridges, railroads, skyscrapers, and steamships. Machinery, tools, and hardware, from the phonograph needle to the steam shovel, are made of steel and iron. Yet, along with its outstanding advantages—its vast supply, its strength, and its low cost—iron has one serious weakness. It RUSTS and CORRODES. It will in time be completely converted into rust unless it is carefully protected.

Until little more than a generation ago, the only method of preventing the rusting and corrosion of iron or steel was to give it a protective coating which would shield it from water and from the atmosphere. Plating the surface with some non-rusting metal such as copper, tin, or zinc or coating it with paint or varnish helped to some extent but did not solve the problem. It is known that a huge amount of money is spent annually in the United States to replace rusted-out automobile mufflers, and that the total damage caused by the rusting of iron and steel in this country amounts to several billion dollars per year.

CHROMIUM: a Protector of Iron and Steel

In the hope that some more satisfactory way of preventing rust and corrosion than plating or painting could be devised, metallurgical laboratories carried on exhaustive investigation and research. Finally a solution was found. Rusting could be stopped by the ADDITION OF ANOTHER METAL TO IRON. This other metal is CHROMIUM, a steel-gray, very hard metal which, added to cast iron along with a small amount of nickel and copper, reduces the rusting in castings. The uses of chromium-nickel-copper castings include pipe, valves, fittings, pumps, compressors, marine engine cylinders, boiler specialties, and marine castings.

When chromium in sufficient quantity is added to steel, stainless steel, a twentieth-century alloy, is produced. When a stainless steel surface is polished, contact with the ordinary atmosphere produces no evidence of rusting and corrosion. Chromium is the only metal which, alloyed with iron and steel, has been found to produce a condition approaching complete resistance to atmospheric corrosion in iron alloys.

The discoverer of this use for chromium was an English metallurgist, Harry Brearly. The discovery was made in 1912. At the time, Brearly was experimenting to find a steel for lining gunbarrels which would resist the erosion and corrosion caused by the explosives used in guns. Brearly's first alloys contained up to 12 per cent chromium. They could be forged and heat-treated just as ordinary carbon steel, but they were much harder. When they contained about 12 per cent chromium, the alloys showed great resistance to corrosion. Brearly's final alloys were approximately 80.9 per cent iron, 18 per cent chromium, 0.10 per cent carbon, and 1.00 per cent manganese. The first true stainless steels were developed from these Brearly alloys.

What Are Stainless Steels?

The stainless steels are a large group of alloys of iron, carbon, and chromium—although many of them contain, in addition, manganese, nickel, and other ingredients. Altogether, there are hundreds of stainless steels available commercially.

The stainless steels are one of the greatest gifts of the electrochemist and metallurgist. They are easily workable, can be bent, welded, machined, and drawn. Their surfaces have an attractive permanent luster. Lighting fixtures, store and window fronts, moldings, window frames, furniture, entrance doors, and grillwork made of stainless steels are found in many modern buildings. The Empire State Building, third tallest structure in the world, with its roots in the bed-rock of the earth and its top often hidden by low clouds, consumed more than 100,000 square feet of polished, rust-defying stainless steel trim.

In the home, stainless steels will be found in cutlery, kitchen utensils, work tables, sinks, etc.

Although the metal chromium was discovered in 1797 by the French chemist Vauquelin, it was not possible to produce stainless steel until the electric furnace was developed on a commercial scale at about the turn of the century. Electricity furnished the high temperature, impossible with coal or oil, necessary to melt chromium, and made it possible to produce chromium alloys in quantity.

Chromium Alloys

Chromium imparts an amazing strength and hardness to steel. A 14-inch shell blasted from a naval gun has the striking force of a runaway locomotive traveling at top speed. Such a shell must have a nose so hard and tough that, although the tremendous impact is centered upon its point, it will pierce the hardest and toughest armor plate without being badly deformed itself.

Chromium occurs in nature only in combination with other elements. Its principal ore is chromite, basically an oxide of chromium, iron, aluminum, and magnesium. Chromium is obtained from its ores by reduction and electrolysis. Over half of all the chromite mined is used for alloying purposes, about one-third goes into re- fractories, and the remainder is taken by chemical and paint manufacturers.

The electric furnace is used to make many useful chromium alloys. Chromium alone may be alloyed with steel, or it may be used with nickel, vanadium, molybdenum, or manganese. Ball bearings, tools, dies, projectiles, the armor plate on army tanks and naval vessels, streamlined railway cars and locomotives, various automobile parts, cutlery—these and countless other things are built of chrome steels.

There are many chromium alloys. The heating element in an electric flatiron, electric stove, or toaster is NI-CHROME, an alloy of the purest nickel and chromium available. Chromium-silicon steels are used for springs and for valves for internal combustion engines. The knife blade that prepares your grapefruit is a chromium alloy.

Not a single ton of steel is made today without using chromium, manganese, molybdenum, tungsten, or some other alloying metal. The steelmaker fills his prescription for steel which is stronger, tougher, harder, or more resistant to wear, heat, and corrosion by adding alloying metals. The results vary according to which alloy metal is used and how much of it is used. An automobile has over one hundred different kinds of steel in it. Each has a special characteristic contributed by alloys. The average home contains about two tons of steel, to be found in everything from sewing needles and bed springs to kitchen knives and refrigerators. All of this steel contains one or more alloys which were extracted from stubborn ores in an electric furnace.

CARBORUNDUM

Modern abrasives (substances used for grinding and polishing), known under such trade names as Carborundum, Crystolon, Carboloy, Exolon, Electrolon, Alundum, Aloxite, and Borolon and almost as hard as diamond, are produced in the intense heat of the electric furnace. These artificial abrasives, made by the electrochemist, have revolutionized machine shop practice. With them, steel and iron can be GROUND to accurate dimensions more quickly than they can be cut. To go into detail in describing the uses of artificial abrasives would be to enumerate thousands of metal products manufactured with their help. The bearings in your bicycle or automobile, the crankshaft, pistons, camshafts, cylinders, piston rings, and wrist pins are ground true and smooth

Carborundum is an artificial abrasive, almost as hard as diamond, which is used to grind materials to accurate size and finish. Carborundum is made in an electric furnace by passing a heavy electric current through a mass of coke, sand, sawdust, and salt. A temperature of 2,700 to 4,000 degrees F is reached. The chemical name of Carborundum is silicon carbide.

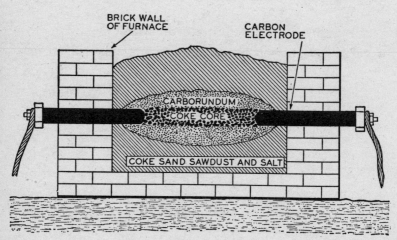

BRICK WALL OF FURNACE

CARBON ELECTRODE

CARBORUNDUM

COKE CORE

COKE SAND SAWDUST AND SALT

with electric furnace abrasives. If the grinding machinery were removed from machine shops, tool-making plants, locomotive works, automobile factories, wherever tough materials must be brought to accurate size and finish, our whole industrial system would be paralyzed.

A small iron pot in a little shop in Monongahela City, Pennsylvania, where Edward G. Acheson was experimenting, was the cradle of the important artificial abrasive industry. When sixteen years old, Acheson went out into the world to earn his own living. He entered the employ of Thomas A. Edison at Menlo Park, New Jersey, at the time Edison was developing the incandescent lamp. After working in the laboratory for a time, Acheson installed Edison electric light plants in Italy, Belgium, and Holland. When he returned to America in 1883, he started to experiment for himself.

Edison's young assistant had pondered for a long time the possibility of finding a material harder than emery which could be used for grinding purposes. He knew that the hardening agent in steel is carbon and that carbon in crystallized form is diamond, the hardest substance known. He decided to experiment, to impregnate clay with carbon under the influence of electric heat in the hope of producing an artificial abrasive.

Acheson filled an iron pot, like the one plumbers use for holding their melted solder, with a mixture of clay and powdered carbon. The pot was attached to one lead from a dynamo, and an arc-light carbon attached to the other end was inserted in the mixture. Current was passed through the contents of the pot until the clay was heated to a very high temperature and melted. Then, when the current had been shut off and the mass in the pot had cooled, it was carefully examined. At first the results seemed disappointing, but then Acheson noticed a few bright specks on the end of the arc-light carbon that had been in the mixture. He found that these shining specks would cut glass as a diamond would. He collected enough of the material to test its abrasive qualities. It proved hard enough to cut the polished face of the diamond in a finger ring.

Under the impression that his discovery was a substance composed of carbon and corundum (a crystalline mineral found in India, Asia Minor, and South Africa), Acheson called the new substance "Carborundum." Subsequent analyses showed the product to be silicon carbide. Thoroughly encouraged, Acheson built a small furnace of bricks, and after much more experimenting he produced enough of the new abrasive to take it to the lapidaries in New York City. He sold the Carborundum by the carat at a rate that would amount to $880 per avoirdupois pound. Later, when Carborundum was produced on a large scale, the price of some forms dropped to fifteen cents a pound.

Acheson set up a factory at Niagara Falls, where today huge electric furnaces 8 feet wide, 8 feet high, and 47 feet long produce Carborundum.

In a modern Carborundum furnace the electrical energy is converted into heat by passing the current directly through a charge of coke, sand, sawdust, and a small amount of salt. The sawdust makes a porous mixture, so that the gases which are generated can escape more easily, while the salt helps to eliminate some of the impurities present in the sand and coke. When the current is turned on, the electrical energy (approximately 2,000 horsepower) heats up the mixture like a huge incandescent lamp filament. A temperature of 2,700 to 4,000 degrees F is reached. The furnace is operated for thirty-six hours, and then, when it has cooled, its brick walls are torn down and its contents unloaded. About 13,000 pounds of crystalline silicon carbide (Carborundum) and 4,000 pounds of silicon-carbide firesand result.

The blue, black, and green iridescent crystals of Carborundum are very hard—next to diamond in hardness. They are crushed and refined into various sizes for fabrication into grinding compounds, stones, wheels, and various shapes.

When the abrasive grains are pressed into the form of a wheel or stone, they are held together by a bond. The principal bonds are ceramic clays, synthetic resins, shellac, rubber, and silicate of soda. The crushed silicon carbide is mixed with the bonding material and pressed into molds. After molding, wheels are baked at high temperatures and given a speed test and trued if necessary. Then they are ready for shipment. Carborundum wheels, stones, and abrasive cloths are black or gray.

Fused Aluminum Oxide

Grinding wheels, stones, abrasive cloths, etc., which have uses similar to those made from Carborundum are made from fused aluminum oxide. This artificial abrasive,

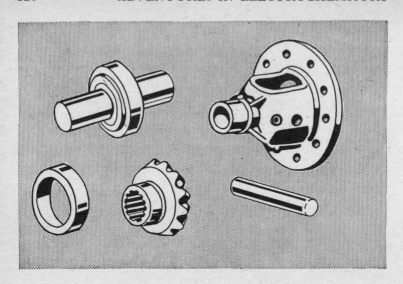

INTERCHANGEABLE PARTS

Millions of bearings, gears, and other machine parts are accurately finished to $\frac{1}{1000}$ of an inch or less by grinding with wheels made of artificial abrasives. Interchangeable parts for automobiles, etc., can be finished to precision dimensions more cheaply and accurately by grinding than by other methods. The stones and abrasives used for polishing and for sharpening tools are also usually electric furnace products.

which is made in an electric furnace, is artificial emery known under the trade names of Alundum and Aloxite.

The crystalline aluminum oxide found in nature is corundum. If transparent and blue it is sapphire. If transparent and red it is ruby. When brown or black it is emery. Alundum is made from bauxite in 10-ton batches in an electric furnace. Bauxite is a hydrated aluminum oxide containing some iron, silica, and titanium. Bauxite of this type is found in nature. The furnace is a circular water-cooled steel shell lined with a wall of alumina. Two large graphite electrodes dip into the bauxite placed in the furnace. A current of about 4,000 amperes at 130 volts is passed through the bauxite charge for 24 hours, changing it into a mass of fused alumina. The ferro-silicon impurities settle at the bottom; the fused alumina floats on top. When it has cooled, the alumina is broken and crushed by machinery and washed and purified by chemical treatment. It is then made into wheels, stones, abrasive cloths, and abrasive powders by methods similar to those used in making the equivalent Carborundum products. Fused alumina is used also in making heat-resisting crucibles and linings for furnaces.

A pure white, chemically pure alumina is also fused and crystallized by the same electric furnace process. Wheels made from this white abrasive cut, without heating, the metal being ground, much as other grinding wheels do.

BORON CARBIDE

Heating boron oxide with carbon in an electric furnace produces a black substance called boron carbide. It is harder than Carborundum, tungsten carbide, or fused alumina. In powder or granular form it is used as a special-purpose abrasive. When heated to a high temperature under pressure, it can be molded. The nozzles for sandblasting equipment are made of molded boron carbide. They are harder than metal nozzles and last longer.

CALCIUM CARBIDE

The manufacture of the gray, stonelike compound of calcium and carbon which is called calcium carbide is a large industry. Since this useful compound is produced in the electric furnace, its manufacture is an electrochemical industry.

Calcium carbide was first discovered by the German chemist, Wöhler, in 1862, but its present-day manufacture is the result of accident and lack of chemical knowledge on the part of a Canadian electrical engineer named Thomas Willson.

Early in the last decade of the nineteenth century, Willson organized a company which hoped to produce aluminum by reducing alumina with carbon in an electric furnace. The money to finance experiments and purchase a small power plant at Spray, North Carolina, was subscribed by the stockholders.

Willson knew very little about chemistry and had to proceed entirely by experiment and by "trial and error." Eventually he produced aluminum, but it was scattered through the charging mixture in the form of tiny globules which would not flow together so that the metal could be tapped from the furnace. Willson was convinced that the method was not practical and changed his plans. He decided to produce calcium from lime and use the calcium to make aluminum. He charged his furnace with a mixture of lime and carbon, hoping that the oxygen of the lime (calcium oxide) would combine with the carbon and leave calcium. But the experiment was a failure; it produced no calcium. When the furnace had cooled, its contents were thrown into the yard. It was raining. One of the workmen in the plant lit his pipe and carelessly threw the still-burning match on the heap of black, stonelike material just discarded. He was amazed when the heap caught fire and burned with bright yellow, smoky flames. Competent chemists were called into consultation. The stones proved to be CALCIUM CARBIDE. The flames were a burning gas called ACETYLENE which was generated by the wet carbide.

CALCIUM CARBIDE "AMMUNITION"

The black powder called "Bangsite" with which many boys are familiar for use in "Big-Bang" gas cannons and "Pop-Guns" is calcium carbide. "Big-Bangs" are harmless. They work as an automobile engine does, using gas, air, and a spark. Bangsite, when wet, changes to acetylene gas and lime. The gas burns in the gun with a harmless bang. It is ignited by a spark from a cerium-iron flint. The gas is not poisonous. Bangsite cannot be set off by concussion or the hottest flame. The limewater formed in the guns will not "eat" into clothing.

Acetylene

When calcium carbide is mixed with water, a violent effervescence occurs. The calcium carbide disintegrates;

a precipitate of calcium hydroxide, and the hydrocarbon (hydrogen and carbon) gas called ACETYLENE are formed. In a suitable burner, acetylene produces a brilliant white, diffusive light. For many years acetylene was used in miners' lamps, in domestic lighting systems, and on carriages. The early automobiles illuminated the road with lamps which burned acetylene. Fifty years ago it was the ambition of almost every boy to have an acetylene lamp for his "wheel," as the bicycle was popularly called at that time.

About 1902 acetylene found use in connection with oxygen for cutting and welding metals by means of the oxyacetylene torch or blow-pipe. This application has grown by leaps and bounds with every passing year. There is only one way to cut apart old steel or iron work quickly, and that is with an oxyacetylene torch.

Acetylene may be stored in steel tanks. The tanks are filled with a porous material saturated with a liquid called acetone. When under pressure, a great deal of acetylene will dissolve in acetone. When the pressure is released, the acetylene escapes from the acetone.

The torches used for cutting and welding burn a mixture of oxygen and acetylene. Oxygen may also be stored in steel tanks. The two gases are kept separate until they arrive at the torch nozzle through separate rubber tubes. Mixed in proper proportion at the torch nozzle, they burn with an intensely hot flame having a temperature of about 6,000 degrees F. The flame of an ordinary gas range used for cooking is only about 2,000 to 2,700 degrees F.

Since ordinary steel melts at about 2,300 degrees F, it quickly gives way under the assault of an oxyacetylene flame. A cutting torch will splutter through a steel beam as fast as a man can cut a wooden timber of the same size with a sharp handsaw.

Oxyacetylene welding, in which the intense heat is employed to melt and flow together the edges of two adjoining pieces of metal, is widely used in industry. The garage man uses it in repairing automobiles. Ships, tanks, bridges, metal furniture, teakettles, filing cabinets, refrigerators, and thousands of other articles are welded either by oxyacetylene or by an electric arc during the process of manufacture.

It was soon found that acetylene is an excellent starting point for producing many synthetic chemicals, such as antifreeze materials, alcohols, artificial rubber, and lacquer solvents. From acetylene, synthetic rubber can be made. Alcohol, glycols, a whole host of substances can be built up or synthesized from acetylene. The manufacture of calcium carbide is an important industry. Nearly 300 million tons of calcium carbide are produced annually.

Cyanamide

Not long after it was found that calcium carbide could be produced in an electric furnace, it was discovered that when nitrogen is passed over calcium carbide heated white-hot, the nitrogen is absorbed and forms calcium cyanamide. This is a compound of calcium, carbon, and nitrogen having the chemical formula $CaCN_2$, sometimes known as NITRO-LIME. It is an excellent fertilizer, since it supplies both calcium and nitrogen to the soil.

In the Cyanamid Process, about two tons of granulated calcium carbide is placed in a large steel drum. The center of the carbide charge is heated by an electrically heated carbon rod, and nitrogen is fed into the drum for about fifty hours. The process transforms all the calcium carbide into calcium cyanamide.

When calcium cyanamide is treated with super-heated steam, the cyanamide is decomposed. One of the useful products formed is ammonia. Calcium cyanamide can also be used as the starting point in the manufacture of nitric acid and urea. Urea is used in the production of urea-formaldehyde plastic resins. Two other important organic compounds, GUANIDINE and DICYANDIAMIDE also are produced from CYANAMIDE as the starting point.

35,000-HORSEPOWER FURNACES

The method of manufacturing calcium carbide today is essentially the same as that discovered by Thomas Willson, but the furnaces are much larger and the process has been somewhat refined. Willson's "big" furnace consumed 800 horsepower; its production was intermittent. It was allowed to cool at the end of each run and was then recharged. Modern carbide furnaces consume 35,000 horsepower, and the operation is a continuous one. The furnace is built in the shape of a huge drum. The charging materials are thrown into one side and the finished product removed on the other.

Some Products of Electric Furnace and Electrolytic Cell *

PRODUCT	RAW MATERIAL	APPLICATIONS OF PRODUCT
Alumina, fused	Bauxite, natural aluminum oxide	Abrasives and refractories
Ammonium persulfate	Ammonium sulfate and sulfuric acid	Photography
Alumina, pure	Bauxite	Insulating material, aluminum metal
Aluminum metal	Bauxite	Light-weight alloys, electric power transmission cables, deoxidizing agent in steel-making, aluminothermal reactions (thermite), ammonal (explosives) acid containers, cooking utensils, protective coatings
Beryllium	Beryl	Light alloys
Bismuth	Lead refining slimes	Alloys
Boron carbide	Boron oxide and carbon	Abrasives
Cadmium	Zinc electro winning slimes	Alloys, electroplating
Calcium	Calcium chloride	Special uses; getters in radio tubes, lamps
Calcium carbide	Lime and coke	Acetylene for welding, cutting, and lighting; acetone, acetic acid, alcohol and synthetic rubber manufacture; airplane dope; calcium cyanamide
Calcium cyanamide	Calcium carbide and nitrogen	Fertilizer, manufacture of ammonia, nitric acid, urea, guanidine and dicyandiamide
Carbon bisulfide	Coke and sulfur	Solvent, insecticide, carbon tetrachloride, artificial silk (viscose)

* Based on the list published in *Industrial Electrochemistry,* by C. L. Mantell, by permission of the McGraw-Hill Book Co.

Products of Electric Furnace and Electrolytic Cell (cont.)

PRODUCT	RAW MATERIAL	APPLICATIONS OF PRODUCT
Caustic soda (sodium hydroxide)	Water and salt	Soaps, pulps, paper, rayon, cellulose film production, petroleum refining, explosives
Cerium metals	Rare earth chlorides	Pyrophoric alloys, cigarette lighters, tracer bullets and shells
Chlorine	Water and salt	Silicon tetrachloride, chlorbenzol, detinning, plastics, hydrochloric acid, oil refining, sanitation, insecticides, disinfectants, water purification, gas warfare, mustard gas, phosgene, chloropicrin
Chrome yellow	Lead and chromium	Paint pigment
Chromium	Chromium ores	Stainless steel, more than 200 alloys
Copper, pure	Crude copper or copper ores	Electrical conductors, brass, bronze, alloys, electroplating, insecticides
Ferro chrome	Chromium ore	Special and high-speed steels, armor plate, projectiles
Ferro manganese	Manganese ore and coke	Steelmaking and production of permanganates
Ferro molybdenum	Molybdenum ore	Special steels
Ferro silicon	Iron, silica rock, coke	Steel manufacture, hydrogen production
Ferro silicontitanium		Steel deoxidizer
Ferro titanium	Titanium ore	Scavenger and inhibitor of grain growth in steel manufacture
Ferro tungsten	Tungsten ore	Imparts great hardness to steel
Ferro vanadium	Iron vanadate	Imparts high-temperature hardness and strength and fine grain to steel
Frary metal	Alkaline earth chlorides	Bearing alloys

PRODUCT	RAW MATERIAL	APPLICATIONS OF PRODUCT
Gold	Copper refining slimes	Jewelry, coinage, and industrial alloys
Graphite	Anthracite coal	Electrodes, motor brushes, lubricants and paints
Hydrogen	Water, sodium hydroxide	Hydrogenated oils and fats, ammonia and hydrochloric acid manufacture, blow torches, chemical reduction processes
Hydrogen peroxide	Ammonium sulfate and sulfuric acid	Antiseptic, bleaching, oxidizing agent
Iron, pig	Iron ore	Steel industry
Iron, pure or "Swedish"	Pyrrhotite	Tubes and special steels, magnetic cores
Lead, refined	Crude lead	Alloys, fittings, acid chambers
Lithium metal	Lepidolite, lithium salts	Light alloys
Magnesium metal	Magnesium chloride	Light-weight alloys, flashlight powders, tracer bullets and flares
Manganese	Manganese ore	Scavenger and deoxidizer in steelmaking, oxidizing agent in chemical industry and in dry-cell batteries
Nickel, refined	Crude nickel	Alloys, electroplating, dairy equipment, imparting hardness, tensile strength and useful magnetic qualities to steel
Nitric acid	Air	Explosives, fertilizers, miscellaneous chemical uses
Oxygen	Water, sodium hydroxide	Oxywelding, oxycutting, medicine, steel converter
Ozone	Air	Sterilization of water, sanitation
Palladium	Nickel refining slimes	Industrial alloys, electrical contact points, dentistry and medicine, jewelry
Perborates	Borax	Bleaching agents for textiles
Phosphoric acid	Phosphate rock, coke and sand	Acid phosphates, cleaners, food products

Products of Electric Furnace and Electrolytic Cell (cont.)

PRODUCT	RAW MATERIAL	APPLICATIONS OF PRODUCT
Phosphorus	Phosphate rock, coke and sand	Matches, phosphor bronze, phosphorus compounds
Platinum	Copper refining slimes	Chemical compounds, electrical contact points, dentistry, medicine, jewelry, catalytic processes, industrial alloys
Potassium chlorate	Potassium chloride	Primers, matches, dyeing
Potassium permanganate	Potassinum manganate	Disinfectant, bleaching, volumetric analysis
Quartz, fused	Quartz rock	Silica tubes, heat-resisting materials, optical uses, prisms, lenses
Rhodium	Nickel refining slimes	Industrial alloys, plating
Silicon	Sand and coke	Silicon steel, resistance units, silicides, silicon tetrachloride, transistors
Silicon carbide	Sand, sawdust and coke	Abrasives and refractories
Silver	Copper refining slimes	Jewelry, tableware, coinage, industrial alloys, photographic chemicals
Sodium bichromate	Chromium salts	Dyeing, tanning
Sodium hypochlorite	Water and salt	Disinfectants, bleaches
Sodium metal	Salt	Used to produce compounds of other elements, ethyl gasoline, dyes, drugs, synthetic rubber, sodium lam
Sodium perchlorate	Sodium salts	Fireworks
Tin, refined	Impure tin, tin dross	Plating, bronzes, alloys
Titanium	Titanium sponge	Fluxes and coatings for welding rods
White lead	Lead	Paint pigment
Zinc	Zinc ore	Alloys, brass galvanizing

Chapter Eight

An Interesting List of Metals

IMMERSION PLATING ·
THE LEAD TREE · THE SILVER TREE

The chemistry of the metals is intimately connected with electrical phenomena. The electrons in the outer shell of a metallic atom are held in place by the attraction of the atom's positive nucleus. This attraction varies a great deal in magnitude in different elements. It is much less in the alkali metals (lithium, sodium, potassium, rubidium, cesium) than in the heavier metals such as platinum, gold, and copper. In the atoms of all metals, however, there is some inclination for the outer electrons to escape and, in so doing, to convert the atom into a positive ION. This conversion can be brought about by an electric current, by contact with other elements, and, in some cases, by exposure to light and to high temperatures.

Metals react with other elements by giving up electrons and becoming positively charged ions. Since the attraction between the outer electrons and the nucleus varies in magnitude in the different elements, the rate at which they enter into chemical reaction also varies. For example, metallic sodium loses its outermost electron very easily. Consequently, it reacts very rapidly with water at room temperature and forms hydrogen gas and a solution of sodium hydroxide. Magnesium does not give up electrons so readily as sodium, and will not react with water unless the water is boiling. On the other hand, copper atoms, which are quite reluctant to give up electrons in comparison with sodium and magnesium, will not react with water at any temperature. In other words, sodium is more active chemically than magnesium, and both sodium and magnesium are more active than copper.

A list of the common metals, arranged in order of their activity, is very useful to the chemist. Such a list is called the Activity Series or Electromotive Series, and appears on a nearby page in this chapter. The most active elements are those toward the top of the list (lithium) and the most inactive toward the bottom (gold). Although hydrogen is not a metal, it sometimes behaves like one in its chemical reactions; it forms a positive ion and is included in the list.

When the metals are arranged in this manner, here are some interesting facts about them.

1. All those from the top down to and including calcium react with cold water, liberating hydrogen from the water and forming a solution of the corresponding hydroxide. Magnesium will liberate hydrogen from hot water.

2. All the metals in the list from lithium down to and including iron react with live steam, yielding hydrogen and the corresponding oxides.

3. All the metals from the top down to and including lead will, theoretically, displace hydrogen from dilute sulfuric or hydrochloric acid, forming the corresponding chlorides and sulfates. This may not always occur from a practical standpoint because some metals form a tough, insoluble, protective coating of oxide on the surface that shields them from acids.

4. Oxides of all the metals from iron down to and including gold can be reduced to metallic form by heating in an atmosphere of hydrogen.

5. Oxides of mercury, silver, palladium, platinum, and gold (at end of list) may be reduced to metallic form by heat alone.

6. All of the metals from lithium down to and including lead (Pb^{++++}) combine directly with oxygen, producing oxides. Those near the top of the list do so with great violence. The metals below mercury may be made to combine with oxygen only indirectly.

7. Any metal in the series will plate out on the metals that precede it in the list.

A chemist has a slightly different way of expressing this last statement. He would say that:

Any metal in the list will displace any metal below it in the list from a solution of a salt of that metal, and will in turn be displaced by any metal above it.

In other words, any two metals in the list will change places under the right circumstances. This can probably be made clear by an experiment which will be described after the next paragraph.

ELECTROMOTIVE SERIES

ELEMENT	ATOMIC NUMBER	SYMBOL	ION
Lithium	3	Li	Li+
Rubidium	37	Rb	Rb+
Potassium	19	K	K+
Strontium	38	Sr	Sr++
Barium	56	Ba	Ba++
Calcium	20	Ca	Ca++
Sodium	11	Na	Na+
Magnesium	12	Mg	Mg++
Aluminum	13	Al	Al+++
Beryllium	4	Be	Be++
Uranium	92	U	U++++
Manganese	25	Mn	Mn++
Tellurium	52	Te	Te−
Zinc	30	Zn	Zn++
Chromium	24	Cr	Cr++
Gallium	31	Ga	Ga+++
Iron	26	Fe	Fe++
Cadmium	48	Cd	Cd++
Indium	49	In	In+++
Thallium	81	Tl	Tl+
Cobalt	27	Co	Co++
Nickel	28	Ni	Ni++
Tin	50	Sn	Sn++
Lead	82	Pb	Pb++
Iron	26	Fe	Fe+++
Hydrogen	1	H	H+
Bismuth	83	Bi	Bi+++
Arsenic	33	As	As+++
Copper	29	Cu	Cu++
Polonium	84	Po	Po++++
Copper	29	Cu	Cu+
Tellurium	52	Te	Te+++
Silver	47	Ag	Ag+
Mercury	80	Hg	Hg++
Lead	82	Pb	Pb++++
Platinum	78	Pt	Pt++++
Palladium	46	Pd	Pd+
Gold	79	Au	Au+++
Gold	79	Au	Au+

Four of the metals, namely lead, iron, copper, and gold, form more than one variety of ion and consequently appear in the list more than once. For example, iron can form ions with either two or three positive charges, as shown in the right-hand column under "ions."

Almost every boy has plated the steel blade of a pocket knife or screwdriver with copper by rubbing it with a solution of copper sulfate. This method of coating one metal with another is known as immersion plating or immersion deposition. The arrangement of the metals in the Electromotive Series indicates which metal will plate another. This will be explained later.

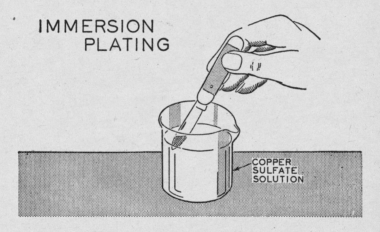

IMMERSION PLATING

COPPER SULFATE SOLUTION

The clean surface of a piece of steel or iron which is dipped into a solution of copper sulfate will become coated with metallic copper.

Die-makers and machinists often use immersion plating when working on steel. They coat the surface of the steel with copper by rubbing it with a rag dipped in a solution of copper sulfate. Marks scratched through the copper and into the steel are more easily visible than marks scratched directly on the steel. Marks are often necessary on steel surfaces to serve as guides in cutting and finishing precision work. Immersion plating is also used to provide sewing needles with gold-plated eyes. The eyes are dipped into a solution of gold chloride. The polished steel surface which comes into contact with the solution becomes plated with a thin layer of gold. Immersion plating is of little industrial importance; it has, however, considerable significance to the chemist.

IMMERSION PLATING

EXPERIMENT. Dissolve two teaspoonfuls of powdered copper sulfate crystals in 6 ounces of warm water. Powdered * copper sulfate is used because it will dissolve more rapidly than large crystals. Brighten the blade of a screwdriver with a piece of fine sandpaper and dip it into this solution. It will become coated with copper and in a few minutes will have a distinct copper color. This experiment is a good example of the displacement of one metal by another. Copper sulfate is inexpensive, and you can readily recognize the copper which plates out on the steel. Before making the next experiment, note the relative positions of copper and iron (we consider steel to be iron in the experiment; it is principally iron and acts like iron.) in the Electromotive Series. Iron is nearer the top of the list than copper, which indicates that it is more

* The crystals are most easily reduced to a powder by crushing in the jaws of a pair of pliers.

active than copper. If a piece of copper is dipped into a solution of iron sulfate, the iron does not plate out on the copper because copper is not active enough to displace iron.

An Immersion Plating Experiment
and an Explanation in Electrochemical Terms

EXPERIMENT. Dip a small strip (4 inches × ½ inch) of clean sheet zinc in the copper sulfate solution for a minute or two. The zinc will become coated with a slimy black coating of finely divided copper. You may conclude from this result that the zinc has displaced the copper.

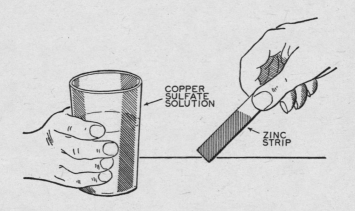

AN IMMERSION PLATING EXPERIMENT

A strip of clean zinc dipped into a copper sulfate solution will become coated with metallic copper.

Explanation. When the zinc acquires its copper coating, some of the zinc goes into the solution and becomes zinc sulfate. The chemical reaction which takes place is written as shown in the accompanying illustration. The same reaction is also shown in chemical symbols.

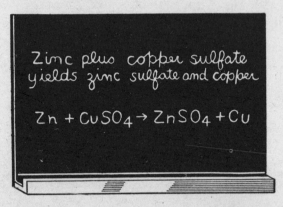

Zinc plus copper sulfate yields zinc sulfate and copper

$$Zn + CuSO_4 \rightarrow ZnSO_4 + Cu$$

THE CHEMICAL REACTION BETWEEN ZINC
AND A COPPER SULFATE SOLUTION

In other words, some of the zinc and some of the copper change places. The Electromotive Series explains why this occurs. Zinc is nearer the top of the list because it is more active chemically than copper. This greater activity gives it the ability to displace copper.

When an atom joins with an atom of another element, each atom tries to secure a complete outer ring of electrons by the smallest possible change. For example, sodium has only one electron in its outer ring. An additional seven electrons are required to give a sodium atom a complete outer ring. But a sodium atom does not try to acquire seven more electrons, because it can LEND the one electron in its outer ring with LESS CHANGE than it can BORROW seven electrons. The atoms of all the metals lend electrons more easily than they borrow them. Some of the metals, like some people, lend more readily than others. An atom of zinc will lend an electron more easily than an atom of copper will.

Electrochemical Language

In a copper sulfate solution there are positive copper ions and negative sulfate ions. When a strip of zinc is dipped into a copper sulfate solution, zinc tries to enter the solution. As the zinc atoms go into the solution and become ions, two electrons leave each zinc atom. The electrons are attracted to the positively charged copper ions. The copper ions are former atoms which have lost two electrons. Positive charges and negative charges neutralize each other. When the electrons (negative) reach the positive copper ions, the charge on the copper ions is neutralized and the copper ions become copper atoms. Copper atoms are neutral and are deposited as metallic copper on that portion of the zinc strip which has not gone into solution. Each of the zinc ions in the solution finds a sulfate ion with which it joins to form zinc sulfate.

"Instant Silver-plate"

By a similar sort of ion exchange process as that just described, copper dipped into a silver nitrate solution will be plated with silver. Silver-plated dishes, bowls, candlesticks, etc., are usually silver-plated copper. This fact is the basis of the "Instant Silver-plate" compounds on the market. If the silver surface on plated ware becomes worn so that the copper is exposed, the copper can be given a "makeshift" silver coating by rubbing it with one of these "plating compounds" containing silver nitrate. However, the only method of putting on a durable coating of silver is by electrodeposition, popularly called electroplating. "Instant" plating compounds for rubbing on a coating of nickel or of chromium are also available, but they also rate as "makeshift" in comparison with electroplating.

THE LEAD "TREE"

Suppose we select two metals, lead and zinc, and perform an experiment to find out whether they will behave as can be expected considering their relative positions in the Electromotive Series. Lead is below zinc in the list and should be deposited on zinc from a solution of a lead salt. Since lead acetate is a lead salt which is readily soluble in water, it is used in the demonstration.

EXPERIMENT.   Dissolve two teaspoonfuls of lead acetate in 6 ounces of warm water. Mix the solution in an 8-ounce glass tumbler and let it stand until clear. Then suspend a small strip (4 inches $\times$ ½ inch) of clean sheet zinc in the solution. Bend one end of the zinc strip so that you can hang it from a pencil laid across the top of the tumbler. Leaflike crystals of metallic lead will grow gradually on the zinc. (Let it remain undisturbed overnight.) A deposit of metal formed in this manner is called a "tree."

Explanation. The "tree" is the result of immersion deposition—the same type of chemical reaction that occurs when zinc becomes plated with copper upon being dipped in copper sulfate solution.

Zinc is above lead in the Electromotive Series. This indicates that zinc is more active chemically than lead. Zinc atoms give up electrons more readily than do lead atoms. When a piece of zinc is dipped into a lead acetate solution, electrons borrowed from zinc atoms go to the positively charged lead ions in the lead acetate solution. The lead ions thus have their charges neutralized, become lead atoms, and are deposited on the zinc strip. The zinc atoms which have lost their electrons go into the solution as zinc ions. There are positive acetate ions in the solution also, and when they combine with the zinc ions, zinc acetate is formed. Thus zinc, since it is more active than lead, displaces lead from lead's own compound.

THE LEAD TREE

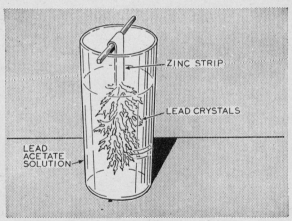

If a strip of zinc is suspended in a solution of lead acetate, leaflike crystals of metallic lead will grow gradually on the zinc and form a "lead tree." Since zinc is more active than lead, zinc displaces lead from lead's own salt.

THE SILVER "TREE"

There are other metals in the Electromotive Series which will form a "tree," for example, silver. According to its position in the series, copper should displace silver from one of silver's own salts.

EXPERIMENT. Silver nitrate is required for this experiment. Since all silver salts are expensive chemicals, the experiment is performed on a small scale.

Dissolve a few small crystals of silver nitrate in about one ounce of distilled water contained in a small test tube or medicine vial. Be careful not to spill any of the solution or get it on your fingers or clothing. Do not handle the silver nitrate crystals with your fingers. Silver nitrate is corrosive and makes black stains.

Fit the test tube or vial with a cork and push a clean piece of stiff copper wire through the center of the cork and into the liquid. Set the tube or vial where it will not be disturbed. In a short time a beautiful pendant of gleaming crystals of metallic silver will grow on the copper wire.

Because copper is more active than silver, it is higher in the Electromotive Series. There are silver ions and nitrate ions in a solution of silver nitrate. Silver ions are positive ions. Copper atoms give up electrons more readily than silver atoms. The electrons given up by the copper atoms are attracted to the positive silver ions and the silver ions lose their positive charge. The silver ions become silver atoms and are deposited on the copper in the form of glistening crystals of metallic silver.

Chapter Nine

Electric Current From Chemicals

THE FIRST BATTERY · INVENTION OF THE

VOLTAIC PILE · AN EXPERIMENTAL PRIMARY CELL

DRY CELLS

Whenever you take the old dry cells out of a flashlight and replace them with new ones, you probably do so as a matter of course. There seems to be nothing unusual about the procedure. An electric flashlight is commonplace today—almost every home has one—and you are most interested in discovering how brightly the lamp will burn with its new battery. You are unaware that for a moment you have something in your hand that represents one of the most important scientific discoveries ever made—the discovery that

AN ELECTRIC CURRENT CAN BE PRODUCED BY MEANS OF CHEMICALS

Electricity has been known for at least two thousand years, but until the first battery was devised, it was known only in the form of frictional, or static, electricity, a fitful, restless thing gone in a flash and good for nothing. Static electricity never stayed long enough for anyone to become well acquainted with it. Until some way of producing a steady current or flow of dynamic electricity was devised, electricity could have no practical application. How could electricity be obtained in a large, steady quantity? That was the problem that confronted electrical scientists before the turn of the nineteenth century. They built various machines which gave a steady supply of STATIC electricity, but this was not the answer.

Chemicals solved the problem, chemicals in the form of a battery which produced a steady current of electricity lasting minutes and hours—long enough so that scientists could get acquainted with it and find out how to put it to work.

THE FIRST BATTERY

The first battery was invented in 1800. It was Volta's "pile," previously mentioned. Here is the story of its devising in more detail. In the years since 1800, practically all developments in electrical science—all those amazing things which have completely altered the ways of civilized living and brought much of the progress in other sciences—have been achieved.

The discovery that an electric current could be produced with chemicals made two men famous. One of these, Luigi Galvani, was a professor of anatomy at the University at Bologna, Italy. The other was Alessandro Volta, professor of physics at the University of Pavia, Italy.

One day in the year 1780, while Galvani was experimenting in his laboratory, an amazing thing happened. He dissected a frog and drove a piece of wire into the frog's backbone. The brass wire touched a piece of sheet iron upon which the frog was lying, and when it did, the DEAD FROG'S LEGS KICKED VIOLENTLY. Galvani, of course, wanted an explanation of such a strange phenomenon. He continued to experiment and found that the same mysterious effect could be produced with other pairs of metals besides brass and iron. Think what a surprise it must have been to this man to be able to cause those

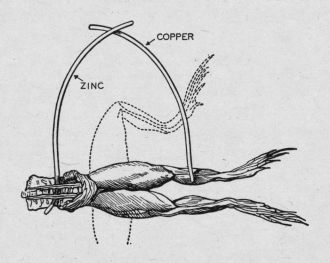

COPPER

ZINC

GALVANI'S FAMED DISCOVERY

The hind legs of a dead frog gave the clue for devising the first battery. Galvani discovered that if a piece of metal is touched to the nerves in a dead frog's backbone while a different metal is laid against the leg muscles, the dead legs will jump and kick whenever the two metals are touched together. Alessandro Volta investigated Galvani's discovery and found that two different metals can be arranged to generate an electric current.

dead legs to move as if alive. Galvani thought that the kicking was due to something in the tissues of the animal; he decided that the nerves of the dead frog generated a "vital fluid," and that when he provided a metal pathway by which the invisible "fluid" could flow between the backbone and the leg muscles, the legs would twitch and kick. He published a scientific paper telling about his experiments and giving his explanation of why the frog's legs moved. The announcement met with great interest among the scientists of the day.

Volta repeated Galvani's experiments with frogs' legs in his own laboratory. Since Volta was a physicist, he possessed knowledge that the anatomist Galvani did not have. Automatically, he used different reasoning in seeking to find out why a dead frog's legs could be made to kick. He centered his attention more upon the metals used in the experiments than upon the nerves and muscles of the frog's legs. He decided that there was no mysterious "vital fluid" involved in the phenomenon, but that the kicks were caused by electricity which was produced by chemical action between two different metals.

THE INVENTION
OF THE VOLTAIC PILE

After more experimenting, Volta found that by arranging several pairs of dissimilar metals in a pile he could build up the small amount of current generated by each pair into quite a strong, steady current. He made the device called a VOLTAIC PILE by stacking up, in alternating order, a number of zinc and copper disks in contact with one another. He placed a piece of cloth moistened with brine between each pair of disks and the pair above it. If the top and bottom disks were touched at the same time a distinct shock was felt. When a wire was connected to the last copper and the first zinc disk, an electric current of several volts was available. The amount of current was feeble in comparison to that produced by a modern battery, but here was the first piece of practi-

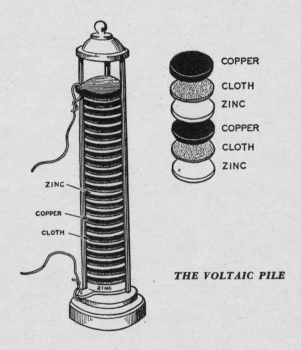

COPPER
CLOTH
ZINC
COPPER
CLOTH
ZINC

ZINC
COPPER
CLOTH
ZINC

THE VOLTAIC PILE

The world's first device for producing an electric current consisted of a pile of alternate zinc and copper disks in contact with one another. A piece of cloth moistened with brine was placed between each pair of disks and the pair above it.

cal electrical equipment in the history of the world. It was the FIRST BATTERY. Current from its terminals would make a dead frog's legs kick violently. It was destined to do much more than this. It began an era of electrical development which has never ceased. In 1800 Volta published an account of his experiments which acquainted the world with his discovery.

When Volta noticed that the electric current produced by his pile became weaker as the cloths between the disks dried, he devised the *couronne de tasses,* or crown of cups, to overcome the difficulty. This consisted of a number of cups filled with salt water. Into each cup were dipped a strip of copper and a strip of zinc. The copper strip in each cup was connected to the zinc strip in the next cup. Experiments soon revealed that the device was

VOLTA'S CROWN OF CUPS WAS THE FIRST PRACTICAL BATTERY

This consisted of a number of cups filled with salt water. Into each cup dipped a strip of copper and a strip of zinc. Experiments soon revealed that the battery was more powerful when dilute sulfuric acid was used in place of salt water.

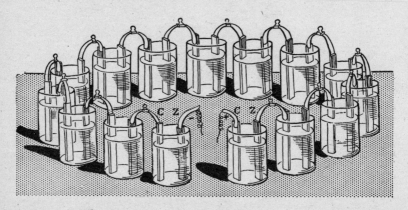

more powerful when dilute acid was substituted for the brine solution. The voltaic pile was the first battery, but Volta's crown of cups was the first PRACTICAL battery. The chemical action between the zinc, copper, and acid in the cups delivered a much stronger electric current than the disks in the pile and, moreover, delivered it steadily for hours. Here was the starting point from which has been developed our present knowledge of how electricity can be useful, how it will create magnetism, produce heat and light, and bring about chemical changes. It was current from batteries that produced the first electric light, ran the first electric motor, telegraph, and telephone.

Since Volta revealed his discovery, other experimenters have devised many different forms of PRIMARY * batteries. But every one of them still retains the principle of Volta's cups in that there must be two different metals or elements and an electrolyte. The zinc and copper strips were the elements of Volta's battery, and the dilute sulfuric acid was the electrolyte.

HOW CHEMICALS
PRODUCE ELECTRICITY

This is a good place to explain the correct use of the words "battery" and "cell." A single unit of a battery consisting of one set of elements and their electrolyte is

* The term PRIMARY battery is used to distinguish the voltaic type, in which the parts which react chemically require replacement when the battery is exhausted, from the SECONDARY, or storage, type. In a storage battery, the initial chemical conditions which produce the electric current may be restored by recharging, that is, by passing an electric current in the reverse direction.

a CELL. Two or more cells, when connected together, are called a BATTERY.

According to present theory, energy is either liberated or absorbed in all chemical reactions. This energy is most often in the form of heat, but in some reactions at least a portion of it may be liberated in the form of light, sound, or electricity. Fundamentally, all chemical reactions in which oxidation and reduction occur are electrical in nature. During oxidation and reduction, complete or partial transfer of electrons from one atom to another takes place. Electrical energy can be produced, therefore, by chemical reaction, the source of energy being the chemical energy stored in the interacting substances.

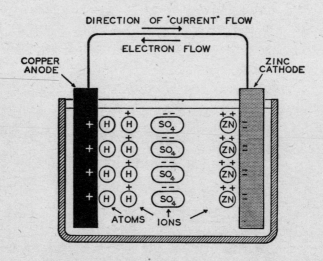

ELECTROCHEMICAL ACTION OF VOLTA'S CELL

A voltaic cell (primary cell) is a chemical device for creating a useful flow of electrons in an electrical path called a circuit.

Electrons are the fundamental particles of electricity. An electric current is a flow of electrons. A primary cell is a chemical device for creating a useful flow of electrons in an electrical path called a circuit.

It has already been explained in a previous chapter that there are positive copper ions and negative sulfate ions in a solution of copper sulfate in water. Also that when a rod of a metal such as zinc is dipped in a solution of copper sulfate, the less active metal is displaced. Each atom of zinc gives up two electrons to the copper ion, and, although there is a transfer of electrons, an electric current is not produced. In order to produce a current it is necessary to prevent the copper ions from coming into contact with the zinc ions in the solution. When zinc goes into solution, forming positive zinc ions, the electrons given up by the zinc must be forced to flow through a wire in order to reach the copper ions and discharge them. This is what a primary cell does.

No primary cell actually creates electricity. It merely provides the energy, called ELECTROMOTIVE FORCE, to push the electrons along in the invisible procession that we call ELECTRIC CURRENT.

In every primary cell there must be one element (called the CATHODE) which will be attacked and consumed by the electrolyte, and one electrode (called the ANODE) which will not react with the electrolyte. In Volta's crown of cups, the copper strips are the anodes and the zinc strips are the cathodes. The cathode element in a primary cell dissolves in the electrolyte, and it is this chemical activity that sets the electrons free.

How to Make a Voltaic Pile

EXPERIMENT.   You can make a voltaic pile by cutting a dozen or more plates 1¼ inches square out of thin copper sheet and an equal number out of sheet zinc. If you prefer to make round disks, as Volta did, make the disks 1¼ inches in diameter (about the size of a fifty-cent piece). Sheet copper and zinc can often be purchased at a tinsmith's or sheet-metal-working shop.

Cut several pieces of blotting paper of the same size and shape as the metal plates. Make half as many blotting paper disks as metal plates. Soak the blotting paper disks in salt water (2 heaping teaspoonfuls of salt in an 8-ounce glass of water).

Solder a copper wire (No. 22 to 24 B.S. gauge) to one of the zinc plates and a second copper wire to one of the copper plates.

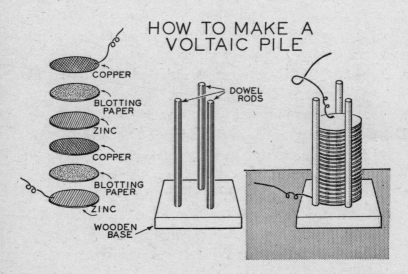

HOW TO MAKE A VOLTAIC PILE

COPPER

BLOTTING PAPER

ZINC

COPPER

BLOTTING PAPER

ZINC

DOWEL RODS

WOODEN BASE

To assemble the pile, start with the zinc plate which has the copper wire soldered to it. Place a piece of blotting paper (wet with salt water) on the zinc and lay a copper plate on top of the blotting paper. Place a zinc plate on top of the copper plate, then a blotting paper, then a copper plate, a zinc plate, a blotting paper, and so on until all the plates have been used. The plates may be maintained in an upright stack by ¼-inch-diameter wood dowel rods driven into holes in a wooden base. The top copper plate should be the one with the copper wire soldered to it.

If a telephone receiver is connected to the top and bottom plates of a pile consisting of only 4 or 5 pairs of plates, the current generated by the pile will make a loud click in the receiver every time the circuit is made and broken. If the pile is composed of 30 or 40 pairs of plates, it will generate sufficient electromotive force to give quite a perceptible but harmless shock when the top and bottom plates are touched at the same time with moistened fingers.

Very little current or amperage is generated by a voltaic pile unless the plates are quite large. In view of the progress made in developing better sources of electric current, a voltaic pile now possesses only historic and experimental interest.

The Defects in Volta's Cell

Ever since Volta invented the cell which is named after him, chemists and physicists have been trying to make better primary cells. Volta's simple zinc-acid-copper cell was soon found to have two defects, called LOCAL ACTION and POLARIZATION.

Bubbles of hydrogen form on the zinc cathode when no current is being drawn from the cell. This means that the zinc is being attacked by the acid and there is, consequently, a waste of both the zinc and the acid. It is called LOCAL ACTION and is to a great extent due to impurities in the zinc.

The second defect is that some of the hydrogen gas which is released when the hydrogen ions give up their charge adheres to the copper and makes the copper anode behave somewhat like an electrode made of hydrogen. A layer of hydrogen is a poor conductor of electricity and weakens the current delivered by the cell. Furthermore, the hydrogen has a slight action of its own, tending to send a current through the electrolyte in the direction opposite from that which carried the hydrogen ions from the zinc to the copper. This also weakens the current delivered by the cell. The collection of hydrogen upon the anode and its effects is called POLARIZATION. Polarization is undesirable, and many kinds of primary cell have been designed to eliminate it.

Carbon as an Anode

One of the first improvements to be made in Volta's original method of making a primary cell was the substitution of carbon for the copper anode. The zinc-copper combination of electrodes delivers a potential of about 1.03 volts per cell, but zinc and carbon electrodes in a cell deliver an electromotive force of 1.5 to 2 volts, depending upon the electrolyte.

LECLANCHÉ CELL

For many years before the turn of the century there were several forms of this cell in practical use for operating electric bells and telephones and, to a limited extent, telegraph apparatus. The Leclanché cell is a zinc-carbon combination in which the electrolyte is a solution of sal ammoniac (ammonium chloride) in water. In the original form, the carbon rod forming the anode was contained in a porous clay cup filled with a mixture of crushed carbon and manganese dioxide. The manganese dioxide acted as a DEPOLARIZER. It prevented polarization, or partially eliminated it, by absorbing the hydro-

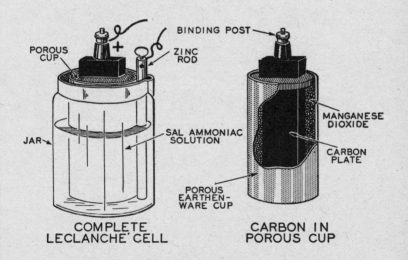

COMPLETE LECLANCHÉ CELL

CARBON IN POROUS CUP

LECLANCHÉ CELL—THE FORERUNNER OF THE DRY CELL

Forms of this cell were once in wide use for operating doorbells, telephones, etc. The Leclanché cell was displaced by the dry cell. The principal difference between the Leclanché cell and the dry cell is in the form of the active ingredient. In the Leclanché cell it is a liquid in the form of a solution of sal ammoniac (ammonium chloride). In the dry cell the sal ammoniac is in the form of moist paste.

gen which tended to collect on the anode. Manganese dioxide is an oxidizing agent. It will slowly give up oxygen if required to do so. This oxygen combines with the hydrogen on the anode, forming water in the process and thus gradually destroying the polarization.

In later forms of the Leclanché cell, the carbon and manganese dioxide, or depolarizing agent, as the latter is called, are molded in the form of a hollow cylinder closed at one end. A zinc rod is suspended centrally in the cylinder. There is almost no local action in a Leclanché cell. It does not deteriorate rapidly when allowed to stand idle. The electromotive force at the terminals, when no current is drawn, is about 1.5 volts, but it falls rapidly if called upon to supply much current.

How to Make a Leclanché-type Cell

EXPERIMENT. The carbon rod for making an experimental Leclanché-type cell may be obtained from an old No. 6 dry cell. Open the cell lengthwise along its side by cutting through the zinc with a hacksaw or with a chisel and hammer. Be careful not to break the carbon. A pint-size fruit or mayonnaise jar will make a suitable container for the electrolyte. Sal ammoniac is a white powder which dissolves readily in water. Use from 2 to 4 ounces of sal ammoniac to a pint of water. The zinc strip should be about 7 inches long and 1 inch wide.

The cell should have a wooden cover provided with a hole and a slot through which the carbon rod and zinc strip will slip. Make the hole so that it is a tight fit for the carbon rod. Paint the wooden cover with melted

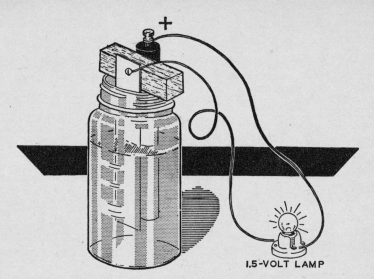

+

1.5-VOLT LAMP

EXPERIMENTAL LECLANCHÉ CELL LIGHTS A 1.5-VOLT FLASHLIGHT LAMP

DETAILS OF EXPERIMENTAL LECLANCHÉ CELL

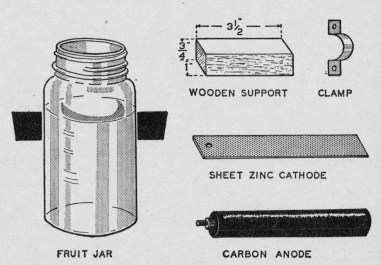

WOODEN SUPPORT   CLAMP

SHEET ZINC CATHODE

FRUIT JAR   CARBON ANODE

paraffin so as to make it waterproof and non-absorbent. When the zinc plate and the carbon rod are slipped in place in the cover and immersed in the solution, the cell is ready to go to work. It will ring a bell or light a 1.5-volt flashlight lamp, and it may be used for performing many electrical experiments. Connection can be made with the zinc strip by soldering a wire to it, or by clamping a wire to the strip with a machine screw and nut. The screw is slipped through a small hole near the upper end of the strip.

No depolarizing agent is used in the homemade cell just described.

ARE DRY CELLS REALLY DRY?

The dry cells in extensive commercial use are a modified form of Leclanché cell. Is a dry cell really dry? No, it is not. If it were, it would not deliver enough current to be of any use. A good dry cell is moist inside. The sal ammoniac solution which forms the electrolyte is held by capillary action in a porous paper lining inside the zinc and in the pores of the depolarizer.

The manufacture of dry cells is a large industry. Millions of the 6-inch dry cells are produced annually in the United States. Billions of the smaller size are sold for radios, flashlights, hand lanterns, and related uses.

If you cut open an old dry cell, you will discover how it is made. The cup or containing jar is a zinc cylinder which also serves as the negative electrode, or cathode, of the cell. The inside of the zinc cup is lined with a layer of absorbent material which may be blotting paper, cheesecloth, or a paste made of starch. A carbon rod placed centrally in the cell serves as a positive electrode, or anode. The space between the carbon rod and the absorbent lining or paste is packed with a depolarizing

A flashlight cell dissected to show what it is made of.

mixture of crushed coke, graphite, and manganese dioxide. The graphite cuts down the resistance of the material
but does not do any depolarizing. The depolarizing mixture and the absorbent material are saturated with a solution of sal ammoniac (ammonium chloride) and zinc
chloride. The top of the cell is sealed with an insulating
cover.

The open circuit voltage of a cell is the voltage measured across the terminals of the cell when the cell is not
in use. The open circuit voltage of the common dry cell
is about 1.6 volts, regardless of size. The voltage is usually considered to be 1.5 volts for practical purposes. The

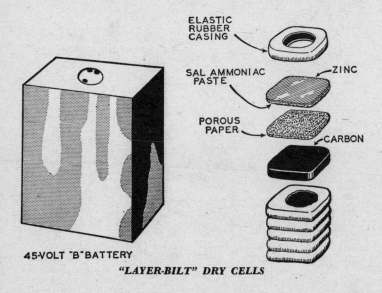

ELASTIC
RUBBER
CASING

SAL AMMONIAC
PASTE   ZINC

POROUS
PAPER

CARBON

45-VOLT "B" BATTERY

"LAYER-BILT" DRY CELLS

The high-voltage (22½ to 300 volts) "B" batteries used in portable
electronic equipment may consist of cylindrical cells similar to flashlight cells or may consist of disks of carbon, zinc, and paper stacked
up like the disks in a voltaic pile. Each cell is hermetically sealed by an
elastic rubber casing to prevent evaporation of the electrolyte.

tiny cells made for a fountain-pen-type flashlight furnish the same open circuit voltage as a No. 6 dry cell which is 6 inches high and 2½ inches in diameter, many times larger than a pen-lite cell. Large cells deliver a greater volume of current than small ones and normally last longer.

Dry cells are not suitable for furnishing large currents. They will supply small currents continuously for a long time, or moderate currents intermittently.

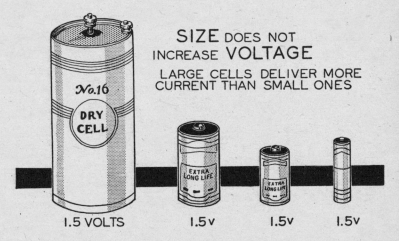

SIZE DOES NOT INCREASE VOLTAGE
LARGE CELLS DELIVER MORE CURRENT THAN SMALL ONES

No.16 DRY CELL

1.5 VOLTS   1.5v   1.5v   1.5v

THE EDISON CELL

For operating railroad signals and furnishing current intermittently in stationary isolated locations where power from a generator is not available, wet primary cells known as Edison cells are often used. They will supply much more energy than dry cells.

An amalgamated zinc casting is used as the cathode. The anode is a plate of compressed cupric oxide (a copper oxide). The surface of the anode is reduced to metallic copper; the cupric oxide under the surface then serves as the depolarizer. The electrolyte is a strong solution of caustic soda or lye which is covered with a film of mineral oil to prevent evaporation.

The open circuit voltage of the copper-oxide-caustic soda-zinc cell is about one volt. There is no appreciable local action, and the cells do not depreciate when standing idle.

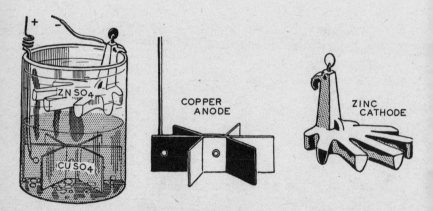

A UNIQUE CELL

This cell, called a "gravity" cell, has two unique features. It utilizes two electrolytes and performs most efficiently when used in "closed" circuits, that is, circuits which require the cell to deliver current almost continuously. Its name is derived from the fact that a concentrated copper sulfate solution is heavier than a zinc sulfate solution, and the two electrolytes are prevented by gravity from mixing. The copper sulfate solution remains at the bottom of the jar, and the zinc sulfate solution floats at the top. A crowfoot-shaped zinc cathode is immersed in the zinc sulfate, and a star-shaped copper anode is immersed in the copper sulfate. Gravity cells were extensively used on telegraph lines for many decades after the telegraph was invented but have now been replaced by other sources of current.

Electric Current from Batteries Is Expensive

Continuous power from any form of primary battery costs about 200 times as much as the same amount of energy would if purchased from the average public utility. But the fact that batteries are portable and will supply current often where no dynamo or public utility is available justifies their cost. The cost of a kilowatt-hour of electrical energy, calculated from the retail price of cells, is approximately $10. The public utility rate for power used in the home averages approximately 7 cents per kilowatt-hour in New York City.

Chapter Ten

Secondary, or Storage, Cells

AN EXPERIMENTAL STORAGE CELL

WHAT IS A STORAGE CELL?

When two lead electrodes are immersed in a dilute solution of sulfuric acid in water and a direct electric current is sent through the solution via the electrodes, a chemical change occurs on the surface of the lead. That portion of the anode, or positive electrode, which is immersed in the electrolyte becomes dark brown or almost black. The color is due to the formation of a thin layer of lead dioxide. The portion of the cathode, or negative electrode, which is immersed in the electrolyte becomes slate gray. Its color is due to the formation of finely divided metallic lead, or sponge lead. The formation of the lead dioxide and the sponge lead is due to electrochemical action.

If the current is allowed to flow long enough for these changes to occur on the surface of the electrodes and the current is then cut off, the result is a SECONDARY CELL.

The electrodes and the electrolyte will now produce an electric current in the manner of the voltaic cell. The arrangement is called a secondary cell to distinguish it from the primary, or voltaic, type of cell. A secondary cell will not produce an electric current until it has been CHARGED by passing a direct current through it.

Two lead plates immersed in dilute sulfuric acid will not produce any current until they have been charged, that is, until a certain chemical condition has been produced on the plates by the electrochemical action of a charging current. The lead-acid type of secondary cell, popularly called a storage battery, which is used in automobiles, airplanes, submarines, power plants, and elsewhere, operates on this principle.

The First Storage Cells

The principle on which all storage cells operate was first observed by a Frenchman named Gautherot. He noticed that silver on platinum wires that had been used for decomposing water with an electric current possessed the power of producing an electric current for a short time when they were immersed in dilute sulfuric acid.

Two or three years later a German experimenter named Ritter made the same discovery and built some experimental secondary, or storage, cells. His arrangement was much like a voltaic pile in construction. It consisted of thin disks of gold separated by cloth disks saturated with a salt solution (sodium chloride). When current from a powerful voltaic battery was sent through Ritter's pile, it was capable, after being disconnected from the voltaic pile, of giving current in the opposite direction for a short time. Ritter made a great variety of storage batteries of this type, employing various metals such as platinum, copper, iron, bismuth, etc. None of Ritter's storage batteries was of practical use. They made interesting experiments and demonstrated a principle, but that was all. More than half a century elapsed after Ritter's experiments before anyone found out how to make a practical storage battery.

Gaston Planté's Storage Cell

In 1860 Gaston Planté greatly improved Ritter's device by employing two plates of sheet lead immersed in dilute sulfuric acid. When the cell was charged by passing an electric current through the plates and the intervening electrolyte, a practical secondary, or storage, cell was produced, capable of furnishing a fairly strong current for a considerable length of time. Like modern storage cells, Planté's cells could be charged and discharged many times. They had only one great fault: a Planté cell had to be much larger and heavier than a modern storage cell of equal capacity.

Modern Lead Storage Cells

In 1880 Charles F. Brush here in America and Faure in France made the same invention—an efficient type of lead storage cell, the one which is in wide use today.

Charles F. Brush was one of the great pioneers in electrical science in America. Born into the world before electricity had been really put to work, this man's name is little known today. But he helped to harness electrical energy and to found the electrical era in which we live. Brush built the first efficient generators, or dynamos, for producing electric current. He perfected the Brush arc light, which was the first electric light to prove practical for street lighting. The first electric lights to be permanently installed for illuminating a public street were twelve 2,000-candlepower Brush arc lamps set up in Public Square in Cleveland, Ohio, in 1879. Soon other cities, stores, and auditoriums adopted them. The Brush Electric Company, which manufactured the Brush dynamos and arc lamps, was one of the four original companies which were subsequently merged to form the General Electric Company. The storage battery which Brush invented cranks the automobile engine and makes it possible for the average person to drive an automobile. Millions of them are in use for this purpose. Brush made his invention too soon to make a fortune from it. His patents expired long before there was a large market for storage cells.

PASTED PLATES

The capacity or ability of the Planté storage cell increased after it had been charged and discharged several times. This process was called FORMING the plates. The original Planté method of forming the plates consisted of charging them alternately in opposite directions several times, that is, reversing the direction of the charging current through the cells. Each successive reversal increased the capacity of the cell slightly, but

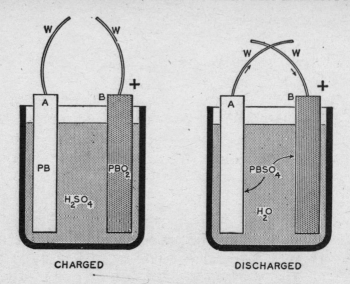

CHARGED   DISCHARGED

ACTION OF THE LEAD-ACID STORAGE CELL

The action of the lead-acid storage cell is chemical in nature. In a fully charged cell, the elements are a spongy lead cathode and a lead dioxide anode immersed in a sulfuric acid solution having a specific gravity of 1.300. In the diagram the elements are shown as single plates. In practice there are usually several negative and several positive plates.

When the terminals of a charged cell are connected together by an outside conductor which provides a path for the movement of electrons between the terminals, the electrolyte becomes strongly ionized. The sulfuric acid dissociates into positive hydrogen ions and negative sulfate ions. The hydrogen ions combine with some of the oxygen of the lead dioxide (PbO_2) of the positive plates and form water. At the same time some of the sulfate ions combine with the lead of the lead dioxide at the positive plates and with some of the sponge lead at the negative plates, forming lead sulfate ($PbSO_4$) in both instances. The negative electrons that have accumulated on the negative lead plates move to the positive plates through the outside conductor which connects the battery terminals. The electromotive force of a fully charged cell under no load is approximately 2.2 volts. As soon as the positive and negative plates are converted to lead sulfate, the cell can no longer produce an electromotive force and must be recharged. The plates can be restored to their original condition and capacity to deliver current by sending a this process was extremely wasteful of current and required several days to accomplish.

Brush's and Faure's invention modified the Planté process so as to decrease greatly the amount of time and current required for forming the plates. In the new process, the lead plates were coated with red oxide of lead before they were subjected to the forming process of passing a current through them while they were immersed in dilute sulfuric acid. By this method, the positive plate was more quickly and highly oxidized into lead dioxide, and the negative plate became covered more quickly with a layer of spongy lead.

So that storage batteries can combine large capacity, small bulk, and moderate weight, the plates of the batteries used for starting and lighting automobiles are not solid lead but are made in the form of a latticework grid filled with a paste made principally of lead oxide. These "pasted" plates are formed in the usual manner by sending a current through them while they are immersed in dilute sulfuric acid. The paste on the positive plates is changed into lead dioxide by the forming process. That on the negative plate becomes spongy lead. There are usually from 11 to 19 grids, or pasted plates, in each cell of an automobile battery. There is always one more nega-

current from an external source through the cell in reverse direction. The charging current ionizes the water in the discharged cell, causing hydrogen ions to unite with sulfate ions of the lead sulfate. This action removes the sulfate deposit from both positive and negative plates. The specific gravity of the electrolyte drops to approximately 1.120 in a fully discharged cell but is restored to 1.300 when the cell is recharged. That is why the condition of a storage cell is often checked by a hydrometer, an instrument that determines the specific gravity of the electrolyte.

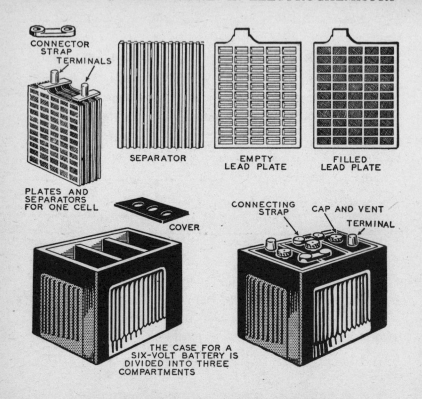

**INTERNAL CONSTRUCTION OF THE "LEAD-ACID"
AUTOMOBILE STORAGE BATTERY**

The plates are cast lead grids. The interstices in the plates are filled with a lead oxide paste. The plates are "formed" by an electrochemical process which reduces the negative plates to sponge lead (Pb), the term "sponge" referring to the softness of the material. The same forming process changes the positive plates to lead dioxide (PbO_2). Each cell consists of a number of positive and negative plates, each group of positive and each group of negative plates being connected together to form a positive or negative group. The positive plates are kept apart from the negative plates by an insulating separator of corrugated wood, perforated hard rubber, or glass cloth. The electrolyte is placed in the cell compartments and water added when necessary through a removable cap and vent. The vent permits the escape of gases formed by electrolysis of the water in the electrolyte during the charging.

tive plate than there are positive plates. The plates are arranged in a compact unit, but the positive plates are kept separated and insulated from the negative plates by separators made of corrugated wood, rubber, or glass cloth. Each 6-volt automobile battery contains three cells. A 12-volt battery contains six cells.

The Chemical Action in a Lead Storage Cell

The active material of the lead storage cell is lead dioxide (PbO_2) on the positive plates and finely divided, or spongy, lead (Pb) on the negative plates. The lead dioxide and the spongy lead are formed by the chemical action which occurs when an electric current is sent through the cell. Electrolysis of the water in the dilute sulfuric acid electrolyte occurs, and oxygen is released at the positive plates. The oxygen oxidizes the lead oxide in the grid and forms lead dioxide. Hydrogen is set free at the negative plate. It changes the oxide on the negative plates into spongy lead. When the cell is discharged, the active material on both the positive and negative plates reacts with the sulfuric acid and is converted into lead sulfate.

When a discharged cell is recharged by passing a current through it, the lead sulfate is converted back into lead dioxide on the positive plates and into sponge lead on the negative plates. In a fully recharged cell in good condition, the lead dioxide on the positive plates is dark brown. It becomes lighter brown when the cell is discharged. The color of the active material on the negative plates is slate gray when the cell is fully recharged. It becomes somewhat darker when the cell is discharged.

The active material on both the positive and negative plates is crystalline in structure and is held together by the intergrowth of crystals. The positive plates "wear" in service by gradually shedding some of the lead dioxide. This falls to the bottom of the cell and forms a "sludge." As fast as the material is shed, however, the exposed surface is oxidized and transformed into lead dioxide by recharging. This process gradually consumes the metallic lead in the structure of the grid, and the latter eventually becomes so corroded that the plate is mechanically weakened. A good set of plates, if not mistreated, is capable of being charged and discharged 2,500 times before its useful life is ended.

There is no actual storage of electricity in a storage cell. There is storage of ENERGY. During the charging process the energy of an electric current is changed into chemical energy. During discharge the chemical energy is converted into electrical energy.

An Experimental Storage Cell

Making this cell will demonstrate the formation of sponge lead and lead dioxide on lead electrodes through the action of a charging current. The electrolyte used in the common lead storage battery is a solution of sulfuric acid. In this experimental cell the electrolyte is a solution of sodium bisulfate. This is recommended to the young experimenter in this instance as a substitute for sulfuric acid in order to avoid the hazards involved in handling the acid.

The following parts and materials are required for making an experimental storage cell:

2 pieces of sheet lead 6 inches long × 1½ inches wide

1 piece of wood 3½ inches × ⅞ inch × ¾ inch

1 1-pint mayonnaise jar

6 teaspoonfuls sodium bisulfate

2 ⅜-inch 6-32 R. H. machine screws

2 washers to fit above screws

2 No. 2 Fahnestock spring contact clip

1 2.2-volt or 2.5-volt, 0.25-ampere flashlight lamp, screw base

1 socket for lamp

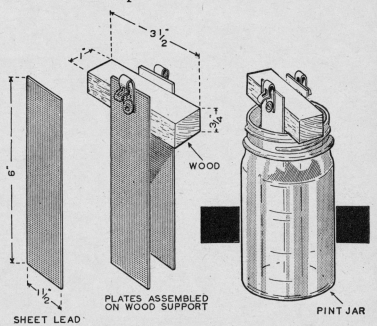

SHEET LEAD

PLATES ASSEMBLED ON WOOD SUPPORT

PINT JAR

AN EXPERIMENTAL STORAGE CELL

Directions for making and charging are given in the text on pgs. 178–182.

CONSTRUCTION. Sheet lead is soft and easily cut with a pair of small tin snips. If it is not over $\frac{1}{16}$ inch thick, it can be cut with household shears without damage to the shears. Clean and roughen the surfaces of both plates by rubbing with a piece of coarse sandpaper. The plates are mounted on opposite sides of the wooden strip. Each plate is held in place by a round-head wood screw and washer. One of the illustrations shows the location of the holes in the plates. The hole nearest one end of each plate is used to mount a Fahnestock connector clip so that a wire may be easily and quickly connected to the plate and also disconnected when necessary. A wire may be connected also by clamping it with a 6-32 machine screw and nut.

The wood strip upon which the plates are mounted should be given a coat of shellac or hot paraffin wax to protect it from the electrolyte. The electrolyte "creeps" up the plates and will permeate uncoated wood and cause a short circuit between the plates.

Mark one of the plates with a plus, or positive, sign. This is to be the positive plate of the battery. Hang the plates in a 1-pint mayonnaise jar. The wood strip resting across the top of the jar will support them. If they have been cut and drilled according to the dimensions in the illustration, the plates will hang just clear of the bottom of the jar. The plates should hang straight and not touch one another.

Dissolve 6 level teaspoonfuls of sodium bisulfate in 12 ounces of warm water and let the solution stand until it has cleared. Then pour this electrolyte into the mayonnaise jar in which the two lead plates are hanging.

The lead plates and the electrolyte are a small storage cell but will not deliver any current until charged. You can prove this by connecting the plates to an electric doorbell or to a 2.2- to 2.5-volt lamp. The bell will not ring and the lamp will not light.

FORMING THE PLATES AND CHARGING THE CELL. Direct current is required to "form" the plates and charge the cell. Direct current can be obtained from a number of sources and these will be explained later. At this time, suppose that four No. 6 dry cells are used. They should be connected in series so that 6 volts is delivered at the terminals. Connect the positive terminal of the dry battery to the lead plate marked with a cross, or plus, sign. Connect the negative terminal of the dry battery to the other lead plate.

A current of about 2 amperes will flow through the storage cell and the charging process will have begun. Notice that small bubbles of gas form on the lead plates. Most of the bubbles form on the negative plate, or cathode. They are hydrogen. The bubbles on the positive plate, or anode, are oxygen. Some of the oxygen at the anode combines with the lead to form lead dioxide.

Charging the storage cell with the current from dry cells is a strain on the dry cells. So, after five to ten minutes, disconnect the storage cell from the dry battery. Notice that the portion of the plates immersed in the electrolyte has changed color. The negative plate is gray; the positive plate is almost black. The storage cell now has a "charge," and if connected to an electric doorbell or to a 2.5-volt flashlight lamp it will ring the bell or light the lamp.

The charge in the experimental storage cell will last only a few minutes. Such a simple storage cell has a very limited capacity. The capacity or ability of the cell to deliver current after it has been charged will increase somewhat if it is charged and discharged several times.

The voltage of a full charged lead storage cell with a sulfuric acid electrolyte is independent of the size of the cell. When measured on open circuit, which means while the cell is not delivering any current, the voltage of a

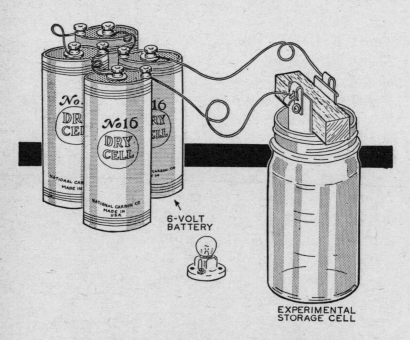

6-VOLT BATTERY

EXPERIMENTAL STORAGE CELL

CHARGING THE EXPERIMENTAL STORAGE CELLS BY MEANS OF CURRENT FROM DRY CELLS

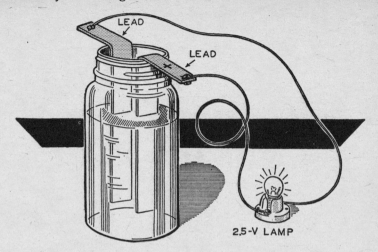

EXPERIMENTAL STORAGE CELL

An experimental storage cell, as illustrated above, can be made from two strips of sheet lead which are bent so as to hang on opposite sides of the jar. The wire connectors are clamped under the heads of two small sheet-metal screws in the upper ends of the lead strips.

fully charged cell is about 2.06 to 2.10 volts, depending upon the temperature and the specific gravity of the electrolyte. The specific gravity of the electrolyte is a measure of the proportionate amount of sulfuric acid mixed with the water.

OTHER METHODS OF CHARGING THE EXPERIMENTAL STORAGE CELL. A 6-volt automobile battery can be used to charge the experimental storage cell. The positive terminal of an auto battery is usually marked with a cross, which is molded in the top of the terminal, or with the abbreviation POS molded in the battery case close to the terminal. Make certain to connect the positive plate of the experimental cell to the positive terminal of the auto battery and the negative to the negative.

A 6-volt auto battery charger can also be used to charge the experimental cell. When the charger is plugged into a 120-volt outlet connected to the house lighting system, it will deliver a direct current of about 8 volts. The charger consists of a transformer, which steps down the 120-volt current, and a rectifier, which changes alternating current into direct current.

When an auto battery charger is used, do not connect it to the experimental cell for more than about fifteen minutes at a time. It is designed to recharge a 6-volt battery, and when connected to a single experimental cell it may become overheated if allowed to operate for more than fifteen or twenty minutes.

Chapter Eleven

Experiments with Electrolysis and the Products of Electrolysis

When an electric current flows through a copper wire, there is no movement of matter in the usual sense, and no noticeable chemical changes take place. The passage of the current in this instance is a process called METALLIC CONDUCTION. On the other hand, when an electric current flows through a water solution containing ions, or through the melted salts of certain metals, there are obvious chemical changes. This process is known as ELECTROLYTIC CONDUCTION. Conduction of an electric current through a chemical compound, with simultaneous chemical changes, is called ELECTROLYSIS. This term is easier to remember when you know that LYSIS is from the Greek word meaning "loosen." Electrolysis is, therefore, "electrical loosening." The electric current loosens the bonds which hold the compound together. The substance which undergoes chemical change by electrolysis is said to be ELECTROLYZED.

A few important commercial processes employing electrolysis have been described in Chapter Six. The amateur can use electrolysis to break up many chemical compounds and will find the experiments interesting. Here are some of the fundamental facts involved in electrolysis:

AN EXPLANATION OF ELECTROLYSIS

In order for electrolysis to take place in a solution, THERE MUST BE IONS PRESENT. During electrolysis, current is led in and out of the solution (or melted salts) being electrolyzed by a positive electrode and a negative electrode, respectively.

Electrodes are neutral; that is, they are neither positive nor negative, and have no effect upon ions until they are connected to a source of electric current. Electrodes can be made positive and negative by connecting them to a source of voltage. Then the electrodes become electrically charged. The anode acquires a positive charge; the cathode carries a negative charge. A positive electrode immersed in a solution in which ions exist will attract negative ions, and a negative electrode will attract positive ions. Electrolysis begins. The ions begin to travel. The positive ions, or cations, move toward the cathode. The negative ions, or anions, move toward the anode. When the cations reach the cathode, they gain, or receive, electrons; and when the anions reach the anode, they lose electrons. By gaining or losing electrons, whichever is necessary, ions become atoms or groups of atoms again. Atoms have no charge; they are electrically neutral.

Some ions and atoms are more chemically active than others. During the process of electrolysis those ions which become comparatively inactive atoms can be captured intact. For example, copper and hydrogen atoms are relatively inactive in comparison with copper and hydrogen ions. Copper ions which lose their charge, thus becoming atoms, are deposited as atoms upon the cathode from a solution of a copper salt. Hydrogen ions exist in many electrolytes, and when they become atoms at the cathode by gaining electrons and becoming neutral, they form bubbles of hydrogen and rise to the surface. On the other hand, ions which react with water, for example sodium and chlorine, form compounds which go into solution.

The Equipment Needed
for Experiments with Electrolysis

The electrodes used in several of the experiments described in this chapter are the carbon rods (anodes) from old size D flashlight cells. The carbons should be removed carefully from the cells with the brass caps still attached. Wash and rinse the rods thoroughly in hot water. Cleansing is necessary in order to remove ammonium chloride and zinc chloride which may be present in the pores of the carbon. Solder one end of a piece of rubber-covered stranded copper wire about 2 feet long to the brass cap on each carbon rod.

Three or four No. 6 dry cells, or some other source of

direct current having a potential of 4½ to 6 volts, will be needed for most of the experiments. Size D flashlight cells can be used but will become exhausted quickly. A 6-volt storage battery is required to operate the electrolytic gas generator when it is used for more than a few minutes at a time. In fact, a 6-volt automobile storage battery will prove more satisfactory than dry cells as the current source for any of the experiments. A used 6-volt auto storage battery which still has enough life for these experiments can often be purchased from an automobile junk yard at a price not beyond the resources of an amateur electrochemist. Binding post terminals which fit a storage battery will make it easy for you to connect wires to it, and they can be purchased at most auto supply stores. A battery charger or rectifier connected to the 120-volt A.C. house-lighting current will keep the battery charged.

WORDS OF CAUTION

Pure water, as you learned earlier in this book, is not an electrolyte or a good conductor of electricity. Adding sulfuric acid to water provides the ions necessary for the electrolysis of water. The reaction which occurs is direct, fairly simple, easily explained, and easily understood.

Several experiments in the electrolysis of water using a sulfuric acid solution as the electrolyte are described in this chapter. These experiments are not intended for young experimenters to perform. Sulfuric acid and its solutions are DANGEROUS and must be HANDLED

WITH CARE. Only high school juniors or seniors or science teachers should demonstrate experiments which use sulfuric acid.

Anyone who uses or experiments with strong, irritating chemicals, with hydrogen generators or with hydrogen gas, should protect his eyes with a plastic eye shield or with motorcycle goggles. You can buy these from an optician. Accidents seldom occur, but there have been times when a slight accident would have been completely harmless if an eye shield had been worn. Safety laws and insurance regulations require the use of safety goggles to protect a worker's eyes in many not very hazardous occupations. Why don't you be careful, too? An injured eye is very uncomfortable.

It is not advisable for an inexperienced or a careless person to mix sulfuric acid and water. *Water should never be poured into acid. Acid is diluted by pouring acid into water. Unless this is done slowly and properly, a violent and dangerous reaction may occur.*

Dilute sulfuric acid can be purchased at some drugstores. Ask the pharmacist to mix 1 fluid ounce of sulfuric acid with 8 fluid ounces of distilled water. The solution should be placed in a bottle fitted with a plastic or rubber closure. If a vegetable cork is used to close the bottle, the acid will soon char and "eat" the cork.

Sulfuric acid is highly active and, even when substantially diluted, will corrode and destroy. It will irritate or burn the skin, char wood, and eat holes in clothing, rugs, and other fabrics. If the acid or its solution is accidentally spilled or spattered, it should be wiped up immediately with an old rag. Then anything that came in contact with the acid should be rinsed with fresh water without loss of time. The next step is to apply household ammonia (dilute ammonium hydroxide) or baking soda (sodium bicarbonate) solution to neutralize the acid. After neutralizing, wash everything that the chemicals have touched.

Unless the amateur electrochemist is old enough and careful enough to handle a sulfuric acid solution without accident, he should skip the electrolysis experiments in which it is used.

The Electrolysis of Water
Produces Oxygen and Hydrogen Gas

EXPERIMENT. Fill an 8-ounce glass tumbler to within about ½ inch from the top with a dilute sulfuric acid solution prepared by a pharmacist by adding 1 ounce of sulfuric acid to 8 ounces of distilled water. Set the tumbler in the center of a soup plate on a porcelain-finished metal tray.

Connect the wires attached to two lead electrodes to the terminals of a battery composed of three No. 6 dry cells in series. Place the electrodes at opposite sides of the tumbler with the lower ends immersed in the electrolyte. Bend the electrodes so that they rest on the edge of the tumbler. The wires on the electrodes should not come into contact with the electrolyte, and the electrodes should not be allowed to touch each other.

Small bubbles of gas will form on each of the electrodes. As they grow larger, the bubbles will break away and rise to the surface of the electrolyte. The bubbles on the cathode form most rapidly. They are HYDROGEN. The bubbles formed on the anode (the electrode connected to the positive terminal of the battery) are OXYGEN. The water is being broken up into the two gases of which it is composed. If the electric current passes through the electrolyte long enough, almost all the water in it will be decomposed into oxygen and hydrogen.

If carbon electrodes are used in this experiment, they may partially disintegrate and turn the electrolyte black. The color can be removed by filtering through filter paper and the electrolyte saved for other experiments.

When lead electrodes are used, the electrolyte will remain clear. Use two strips of thin sheet lead 4 inches

ELECTROLYSIS OF WATER USING SULFURIC ACID SOLUTION AND LEAD ELECTRODES

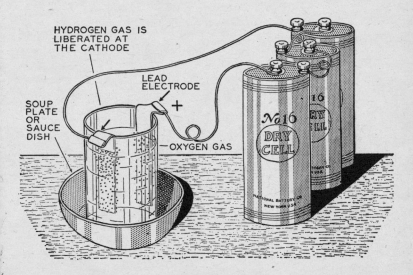

HYDROGEN GAS IS LIBERATED AT THE CATHODE

LEAD ELECTRODE

SOUP PLATE OR SAUCE DISH

OXYGEN GAS

long and ½ inch wide. Connection can be made to the wires by bending one end of each plate around a wire and crimping it with a pair of pliers. Clean the surface of the lead by rubbing with sandpaper.

When lead electrodes are used, some of the oxygen and hydrogen first produced by the electrolysis will be used in bringing about chemical changes on the surface of the electrodes. In a few minutes, however, oxygen and hydrogen bubbles will be formed in considerable volume. Lead electrodes make better contact with the electrolyte than carbon electrodes, so that more current flows through the electrolyte and chemical action takes place at a greater rate.

How to Collect the Oxygen and Hydrogen Liberated by the Electrolysis of Water

The bubbles produced by the electrolysis of water can be collected and proved to be oxygen and hydrogen. Test tubes can be filled with the gas by the method chemists term DISPLACEMENT. A test tube filled with electrolyte is inverted over each electrode. When an electric current passes through the electrolyte, bubbles of gas rise in the tubes and displace the electrolyte. Dilute sulfuric acid is used as the electrolyte. Again the warning is necessary that this experiment should not be performed by any experimenter who is not old enough and careful enough to handle the acid solution without accident. Since it is not easy to invert the test tubes in the electrolyte without spattering it or without letting the fingers come into contact with the solution, the use of a dilute sulfuric acid electrolyte is best restricted to older students of chemistry or to the science teacher.

EXPERIMENT. The apparatus and materials in the following list are needed to perform this experiment:

1   porcelain-finished metal tray
1   soup plate
1   1-pint wide-mouthed glass jar approximately 3¼ inches in diameter and 4 inches high. Some brands of peanut butter are packed in a jar of this type
2   6 inch × ¾ inch test tubes
2   3¼ inch × ½ inch sheet lead electrodes
18 ounces dilute sulfuric acid
4   No. 6 dry cells or other 6-volt direct current source wire for connections, cotton batting, tweezers

Pour about 14 ounces of electrolyte into the wide-mouthed glass jar. Have your druggist mix the electrolyte by adding 2 fluid ounces of sulfuric acid to 16 fluid ounces of distilled water. Place the jar in the center of the soup plate and set the plate on the porcelain-finished metal tray. During the experiment, as the electrolyte in the test tubes is displaced by gas, the electrolyte in the jar will overflow. The soup plate and tray are necessary to catch the displaced liquid.

Bend the end of each lead electrode over so that it can be squeezed or crimped on the end of a piece of No. 18 or No. 20 B. S. gauge insulated copper wire. Cover any exposed bare copper wire with rubber tape so as to insulate the copper from the acid solution. Place the elec-trodes in an inverted position in the glass jar, that is, so that the ends to which the wires are attached rest on the bottom of the jar.

Fill two 6 inch × ¾ inch test tubes to within ½ inch from the top with electrolyte. Stopper both tubes with a wad of cotton batting. Invert both tubes (mouth down) in the jar of electrolyte and remove the cotton stoppers with a pair of tweezers or forceps. This operation should be performed without lifting the test tubes above the

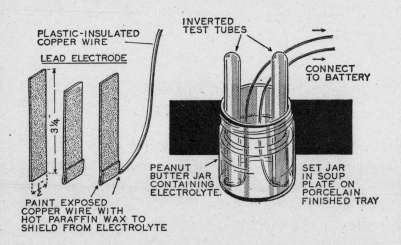

PLASTIC-INSULATED COPPER WIRE

LEAD ELECTRODE

3¼"

½"

PAINT EXPOSED COPPER WIRE WITH HOT PARAFFIN WAX TO SHIELD FROM ELECTROLYTE

INVERTED TEST TUBES

CONNECT TO BATTERY

PEANUT BUTTER JAR CONTAINING ELECTROLYTE

SET JAR IN SOUP PLATE ON PORCELAIN FINISHED TRAY

APPARATUS FOR COLLECTING OXYGEN AND HYDROGEN IN TEST TUBES BY DISPLACEMENT

The electrodes are made of thin sheet lead. Each is connected to the bared end of a piece of insulated copper wire by folding the end of the electrode over and crimping the wire in the fold. Use plastic in-sulated wire. This type of insulation will not be damaged by the electrolyte. The wire may be obtained at a radio repair shop. Any exposed copper must be protected by coating with wax.

surface of the electrolyte so that air can enter. Push a tube down over each electrode so that there is an electrode in each tube and both tubes are filled with electrolyte. A small bubble of air from the cotton that might have escaped to the top of a tube is not objectionable. However, the tubes should be 99 per cent filled with electrolyte. The success of the experiment will depend upon preventing the escape of any electrolyte from the tubes and preventing the entry of any air. If either test tube has a large bubble of air at the top, remove the tube, refill it with electrolyte, and invert it over the electrode again.

Connect the wires attached to the electrodes to a 4½-volt or a 6-volt battery. The 6-volt battery will produce the most gas in the least time. Twice as much hydrogen (at the cathode) will be produced as oxygen, and consequently the test tube of hydrogen will be the first to be filled. As the electrolyte in the tubes is displaced by gas, the acid solution will run over the brim of the jar and be retained in the soup plate.

Hydrogen. The principal characteristics of hydrogen are the readiness with which it burns, and its lightness. When mixed with air in the right proportion, hydrogen explodes with considerable force. It will shatter bottles and narrow-neck jars. However, test tubes filled with hydrogen can be ignited without danger.

Oxygen. Combustion, which takes place slowly in the diluted oxygen of the atmosphere, is greatly speeded up in pure oxygen. A substance which is merely smoldering in air will burst into flame in oxygen.

EXPLODING HYDROGEN

EXPERIMENT. Lift the test tube filled with hydrogen out of the electrolyte. Keep the tube inverted (open and down) and quickly apply a lighted match to the mouth of the tube. The hydrogen will burn with a "plop" or "plurp" sound. In fact, it burns so fast that its combustion is a mild explosion.

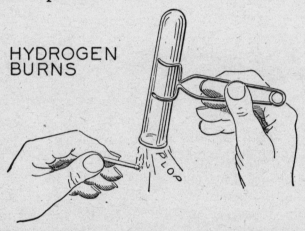

HYDROGEN
BURNS

Speeding Combustion

EXPERIMENT. Have ready a long splinter (9 inches) which is smoldering and glowing red at one end. Lift the test tube which has been partly filled with oxygen out of the electrolyte. Some air may enter the tube and dilute the oxygen, but if you act quickly and carefully, the mixture of air and oxygen will still contain a much greater percentage of oxygen than the atmosphere. Thrust the glowing end of the splinter far into the tube. The splinter will glow more brightly and burst into flame. The increased oxygen increases the rate of combustion.

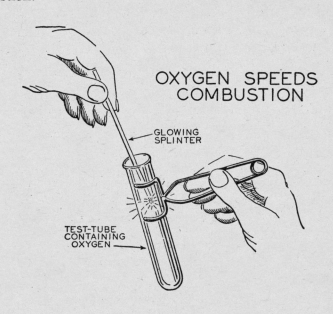

OXYGEN SPEEDS
COMBUSTION

GLOWING
SPLINTER

TEST-TUBE
CONTAINING
OXYGEN

THE ELECTROLYSIS
OF A SODIUM CHLORIDE SOLUTION

Here is salt, an old friend. It has been explained in an earlier chapter that the electrolysis of brine (a strong solution of common salt in water) is one of the most important industrial chemical processes.

EXPERIMENT. Dissolve 4 teaspoonfuls of table salt (sodium chloride) in an 8-ounce glass tumbler or beaker glass nearly filled with lukewarm water. The solution may appear cloudy for a few minutes. When it has cleared, immerse two carbon electrodes (size D dry cell carbons) in it. Connect the electrodes to a 4½- to 6-volt dry cell battery. Three dry cells in series will deliver 4½ volts. Four dry cells in series will deliver 6 volts.

As soon as current flows through the salt solution, bubbles will arise from both electrodes. Tests can be made to show what these bubbles are. We can surmise what they are if we apply the Theory of Electrolytic Dissociation.

In a solution of sodium chloride in water there are positively charged sodium ions and negatively charged chlorine ions moving, or "migrating," through the solution. In addition to these ions, the water provides, through its own dissociation, a small quantity of positive hydrogen ions and negative hydroxyl ions. The solution therefore contains

$$Na^+, Cl^-, H^+, OH^-$$

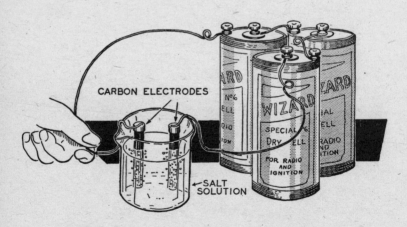

CARBON ELECTRODES

←SALT SOLUTION

THE ELECTROLYSIS OF A SOLUTION OF COMMON TABLE SALT

Hydrogen and oxygen gas are liberated, and a solution of sodium hydroxide and sodium hypochlorite are formed if the current continues to flow until all the sodium chloride has been electrolyzed.

When no current flows through the solution, the ions move around without definite direction. When two electrodes connected to a battery are immersed in the solution, there is great activity. As might be expected, the positively charged ions (Na^+ and H^+) are attracted to the negative electrode (cathode), and the negatively charged ions (Cl^- and OH^-) are attracted to the positive electrode (anode). When a hydrogen ion reaches the cathode, it receives an electron from the latter and thus becomes neutral, that is, bears no charge. Without any charge, it is no longer an ion, but is an atom. When enough hydrogen ions become hydrogen atoms, they form molecules which gather in the form of hydrogen bubbles and rise to the surface of the electrolyte. The sodium ion, which is also attracted to the cathode, is much more reluctant than is the hydrogen ion to accept electrons, unless there is a very heavy current passing through the electrolyte, more current than is supplied by the battery of dry cells.

While the positive ions (cations) have been traveling to the negative electrode, the negative ions, Cl^- and OH^- (chlorine and hydroxyl ions), have been attracted toward the positive electrode. At this electrode, a chlorine ion loses an electron and becomes a chlorine atom. Each two chlorine atoms form one double-atom chlorine molecule (Cl_2), giving up two electrons in the process: and so the chlorine molecules collect, forming bubbles of chlorine which rise to the surface of the electrolyte.

The sodium ions, Na, and the hydroxyl ions, OH^-,

remain in the solution, combine with each other and form a solution of sodium hydroxide, the chemical formula for which is NaOH.

Sniff the bubbles arising from the cathode and you will detect the characteristic sharp, irritating odor of chlorine. Concentrated chlorine is poisonous, but the very small amount liberated in this experiment will not hurt you.

As electrolysis of the salt solution proceeds, some of the chlorine dissolves in the solution and reacts with the sodium hydroxide, forming sodium hypochlorite. Sodium hypochlorite is a useful disinfecting and bleaching agent. A water solution of sodium hypochlorite is often used in the household. A well-known commercial brand, trade-marked Clorox, is sold at grocery stores. The efficient bactericidal agent used in World War I for treating wounds and known as Dakin's solution is a pure solution of sodium hypochlorite. Many paper mills decompose salt in electrolytic cells, to obtain chlorine, sodium hydroxide and sodium hypochlorite. In making white paper, the gray pulp is usually bleached with either sodium hypochlorite or calcium hypochlorite.

The formation of sodium hypochlorite during the electrolysis of a salt solution can be prevented if the ions at the cathode and anode are not allowed to mix. They can be kept separated by surrounding the anode with a porous diaphragm.

The industrial electrolysis of brine employs several types of cells designed to separate marketable products:

hydrogen, chlorine, sodium, sodium hydroxide, and sodium hypochlorite.

The Electrolysis of Sodium Chloride
to Produce Sodium Hydroxide

EXPERIMENT. Make a small cylinder 3¾ inches long, 1 inch in diameter out of asbestos paper. Overlap the edges and seal in place with hot paraffin. Close one end with a circular piece of asbestos paper also sealed in place with hot paraffin. You can purchase asbestos paper at a hardware store.

Place the paper cup in an 8-ounce glass tumbler with the open end up. Connect two carbon electrodes (carbons from size D dry cells) to the terminals of a 4½- to 6-volt dry battery. Place the anode (electrode connected to the positive battery terminal) inside the paper cup and the cathode on the outside. Pour a solution of common table salt into the tumbler both inside and outside the cup until the level of the solution is about ½ inch below the top of the glass. Prepare the salt solution by dissolving 4 tablespoonsfuls of table salt in 8 ounces of lukewarm water.

This arrangement will prevent the ions formed at the two electrodes during electrolysis of the solution from mixing together. When current flows through the solution, chlorine liberated at the anode will dissolve in the water within the porous cup. The water will soon become saturated with the gas; that is, it will be unable to dissolve any more gas. Then the chlorine will rise to the surface in the form of bubbles. Hydrogen bubbles will arise from the cathode. If electrolysis proceeds long enough, the liquid in the glass tumbler surrounding the porous cup will eventually consist of a solution of sodium hydroxide mixed with sodium chloride. Eventually all of the sodium chloride will be decomposed, and a water solution of sodium hydroxide will remain. Dip a piece of red litmus paper into the sodium hydroxide solution. The paper will turn blue. Alkalis turn red litmus blue. Sodium hydroxide is alkaline. The principle demonstrated by this experiment is the same as that used commercially to produce hydrogen, chlorine and sodium hydroxide for industry.

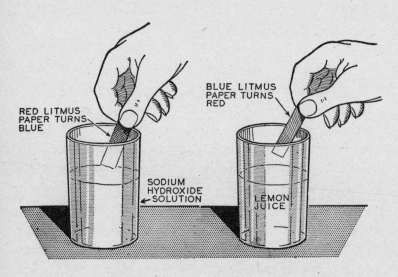

BLUE LITMUS
PAPER TURNS
RED

RED LITMUS
PAPER TURNS
BLUE

SODIUM
HYDROXIDE
←SOLUTION

LEMON
JUICE

A TEST FOR ACIDS AND ALKALIS

Litmus is a vegetable dye. Paper which has been dyed with litmus is used to show by a change in color whether a solution is acid or alkaline. Acid turns blue litmus red. Sodium hydroxide (an alkali) turns red litmus blue.

More about the Chemicals Produced from Salt

It has been explained that five chemicals, namely, hydrogen, chlorine, sodium, sodium hydroxide, and sodium hypochlorite are produced commercially in large quantities by electrolysis from brine. Some of the uses of sodium hypochlorite have been mentioned. Brine is usually obtained by pumping from underground salt deposits.

HYDROGEN. Hydrogen is a colorless, odorless, and tasteless gas. It is the lightest substance known. Water is the sole product when hydrogen burns, hence the name hydrogen, which means "water-producer" in Greek. Commercial hydrogen is sold in steel tanks under high pressure. The annual production is many billions of cubic feet. It has many uses, some of which are described later in this chapter.

CHLORINE. Chlorine ranks with the most important of all chemical elements. It belongs to a sort of family group of chemicals which includes fluorine, chlorine, bromine, iodine, and astatine.* The group is called the HALOGENS, from a Greek word meaning "salt producer." With metals such as sodium and potassium the halogens all form compounds resembling ordinary table salt to some extent.

The importance of chlorine in water purification has been mentioned in an earlier chapter. The largest user of chlorine is the bleaching industry. Large tonnages of chlorine are used to bleach the natural gray or brown color out of textiles and paper. Chlorine also has a multi-

---

* Astatine is a radioactive element, number 85 in the Periodic Table.

tude of uses in the preparation of other chemicals. A few examples are: carbon tetrachloride, hydrogen chloride, tin tetrachloride, the chlorides of sulfur, insecticides, and many others.

SODIUM HYDROXIDE. Annual U.S. production of this chemical is over 10 million tons, produced largely by electrolysis. Popularly it is called lye, although this name is also sometimes applied to potassium hydroxide. Sodium hydroxide solutions feel soapy and are very corrosive to many substances, including human skin. It is a typical alkali, or base, able to neutralize strong acids. The principal use of sodium hydroxide is in the manufacture of other chemicals. It is the cheapest of the very soluble, stable bases and is used in large amounts in petroleum refining, in the manufacture of soap, rayon, paper, textiles, and cellulose film, and in a host of other processes.

SODIUM. Sodium is a soft, silvery metal. It is the chief member of a chemical family of six called the ALKALI METALS. Its brothers are potassium, lithium, rubidium, cesium, and francium. They all find a place in the electromotive series of metals. Each has a single electron in its outer ring which it can lend easily to some other atom. All six alkali metals are exceedingly active.

Usually metals (except mercury) are thought of as substances which are heavy, hard, and difficult to melt. Sodium contradicts this popular conception of a metal. It is light enough to float on water, it is soft enough to be cut with a knife, and it melts below the boiling point of water. It is so active, and it combines so readily with the water vapor and oxygen in the air, that in laboratories it is kept sealed in metal containers or immersed in kerosene.

When a piece of sodium is thrown into water, it reacts vigorously. So much heat is evolved that the metal melts into a spluttering globule which zig-zags around rapidly on the surface of the water. The metal soon disappears. Hydrogen and sodium hydroxide are formed during the reaction of the metal with the water. Frequently the hydrogen catches fire.

Large tonnages of sodium metal are produced for use in the manufacture of tetraethyl lead, dyestuffs, sodium peroxide, plastics, sodium cyanide, and organic chemicals. Additional quantities are used in photoelectric cells, sodium vapor lamps, and connecting rods in airplane engines, and in engineering where heat conduction is a problem.

Sodium metal is produced commercially by the electrolysis of fused sodium chloride. Chlorine gas is produced simultaneously. The equipment commonly used is known as the Downs electrolytic cell. The illustration is a diagram of this cell. The cell consists of an iron box lined with firebrick. A circular iron or copper cathode surrounds a graphite anode which projects upward through the bottom of the cell. A wire gauze partition keeps separated the sodium metal and chlorine gas which are produced.

The principle involved in the electrolysis of fused sodium chloride is a very simple one, but it cannot be demonstrated in the average home laboratory because a strong electric current and a high temperature are required.

An Electrolytic Cell for Producing Larger Quantities of Oxygen and Hydrogen

The simple arrangement whereby oxygen and hydrogen from the electrolysis of water are collected in test tubes does not furnish any considerable amount of gas. By using larger apparatus which operates on the same principle and connecting it to a 6-volt storage battery instead of to dry cells, enough gas can be collected for many interesting experiments. Those with oxygen are especially spectacular and interesting.

A storage battery is needed because dry cells cannot supply the current required for a long enough time.

A 1-pint fruit or mayonnaise jar with an airtight metal screw-cap; two 6 inch × ¾ inch test tubes; two rubber corks which will fit tightly into the pieces of hose; two pieces of ⁵⁄₁₆-inch (outside diameter) plastic tube 2 inches long; and about 4 feet of rubber or plastic tubing to fit over the ⅝-inch plastic tubes are used in building the cell.

In the cover of the jar make two round holes which are a snug fit for the plastic hose. Mark the holes on the cover with a compass or a pair of dividers. Drill a hole in the center of each circle and enlarge the holes with a round file to make a close fit for the pieces of hose. Each piece of hose should be cemented in the cover with melted sealing wax.

The electrodes are two strips of sheet lead, 4½ inches

ELECTROLYTIC GAS GENERATOR

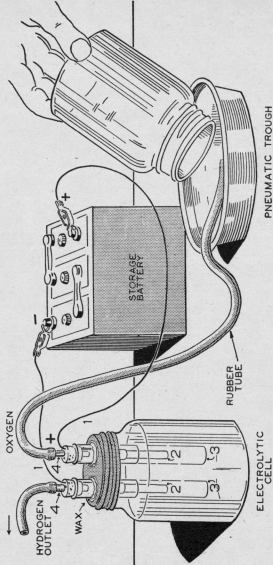

KEEP FLAMES AWAY
FROM GAS OUTLETS

OXYGEN

HYDROGEN
OUTLET

WAX

RUBBER
TUBE

STORAGE
BATTERY

PNEUMATIC TROUGH

ELECTROLYTIC
CELL

Considerable quantities of hydrogen and oxygen gas can be generated with a 6-volt storage battery and an electrolytic cell as shown in the illustration. The gases pass out through the tubes at the top of the generator and may be collected in small jars filled with water and inverted in a pneumatic trough. The rubber tube attached to the hydrogen outlet should be longer than that illustrated. There is not space on the page to show a longer tube. Plastic tubes and tubing are available in many sizes. They do not shatter into sharp fragments like glass.

long and ½ inch wide. An 18-inch length of plastic-insulated hook-up wire (used to wire and repair radio receivers) is connected to one end of each electrode. Plastic-covered wire is used because it is resistant to the acid electrolyte. If any bare copper is exposed where the wires are connected to the electrodes, protect it from the electrolyte by coating it with hot wax.

The electrodes are placed inside the two pieces of plastic hose. The wires connected to the electrodes pass out of the tubes through tight-fitting holes bored through the cork. The jar cover, pieces of hose, glass tubes, rubber corks, and wires must all make an airtight fit so that no gas can escape from the cell except through the small plastic tubes in the corks.

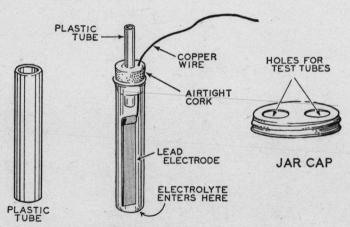

PLASTIC
TUBE →

COPPER
WIRE

HOLES FOR
TEST TUBES

AIRTIGHT
CORK

LEAD
ELECTRODE

JAR CAP

ELECTROLYTE
ENTERS HERE

PLASTIC
TUBE

PARTS FOR THE ELECTROLYTIC GAS GENERATOR

The holes in the jar cap should fit the tubes. The tubes are cemented in the cap with sealing-wax. Tubes, corks, and wires must all be sealed airtight, so that no gas can escape. The lead electrodes are placed inside the tubes. The wires connected to the electrodes pass through the corks in the tops of the tubes.

The electrolyte used in the jar is dilute sulfuric acid made by mixing 2 fluid ounces of sulfuric acid in 1 pint of water. See instruction under heading WORDS OF CAUTION on pages 186–188.

When the cell is connected to a 6-volt storage battery, oxygen collects in the tube enclosing the anode, or positive electrode. Hydrogen collects in the other tube. The gas passes out through the tubes in the corks and may be collected in small jars filled with water and inverted in a pneumatic trough. The gases are led from the cell to the trough through a rubber or plastic tube.

A pneumatic trough is an arrangement for collecting gases which is often used in chemical laboratories. It may be used to collect any gas which is not quickly absorbed by water. The illustration shows how the apparatus is set up. A shallow pan (round cake tin) and some ½-pint jars to collect the gases are required. The pan should be partly filled with water, just deep enough to seal the mouth of a jar when it is inverted in a pan. Not enough gas pressure is generated in the electrolytic cell to overcome the pressure which would be exerted by deeper water.

To collect gas in a small jar, first fill it with water. Cover the mouth with a piece of cardboard so that no water can escape while you invert the jar and set it upside down in the water in the pan. Slide the cardboard out from under the jar without letting any water out or air in. Place the end of the tube leading from the electrolytic cell under the edge of the inverted jar so that the gas can bubble up and displace the water in the jar.

To remove a jar filled with gas from the trough, remove the rubber tube and slide a piece of cardboard under the jar so as to close the mouth. Then lift the jar out of the trough with the cardboard still in place. If it contains hydrogen, keep the jar in an inverted position. Otherwise, as hydrogen is lighter than air, it will escape.

EXPERIMENTS WITH HYDROGEN AND OXYGEN

Because hydrogen is the lightest substance known, it is used in balloons and in so-called "lighter-than-air" craft. However, owing to its great combustibility, it has been largely superseded in American balloons and dirigibles by a non-inflammable mixture of helium and hydrogen. Helium is not as light as hydrogen but has the advantage that it does not burn. Three-fourths of the helium produced is used by the Federal Government, and the balance is used by private industry.

Hydrogen has many practical uses. It produces intense heat when burned and so is a valuable constituent of many gaseous fuels. The oxyhydrogen torch, burning hydrogen and oxygen, develops a temperature of about 5,000 degrees F. Many liquid oils and fats, such as cottonseed and cocoanut oils, are converted into semi-solids when treated with hydrogen in the presence of finely divided nickel. The nickel acts as a catalyst. Crisco and the "nut-butters" are made in this way. Large quantities of ammonia are made by the direct combination of hydrogen with nitrogen.

CAUTION. Do not fill large jars (more than 8-ounce capacity) or any bottles with hydrogen. Use only test tubes, small wide-mouth jars, or, to be perfectly safe, 8-ounce tumblers. When mixed with air, hydrogen is explosive, and if hydrogen contained in a bottle with the right amount of air should be ignited, it would shatter the bottle with terrific force and you would probably be badly cut by flying glass. Hydrogen contained in an 8-ounce tumbler which has a mouth as wide as its base, or in a test tube, merely burns with a sharp "plurp" when ignited. Play safe. Experiments are entertaining and instructive. Don't let any of your experiments be the cause of an accident. AGAIN—PLAY SAFE!

The Lightness of Hydrogen

EXPERIMENT. Fill an 8-ounce tumbler with hydrogen and turn it upright with the mouth uncovered. After two minutes, thrust a blazing splinter into the tumbler. Nothing unusual will occur. Probably the flame on the splinter will be extinguished after a few seconds. There is no hydrogen in the tumbler to burn. Since it is lighter than air, it has escaped upward out of the open tumbler and the space it filled is now occupied by air.

Pouring Hydrogen Upward

EXPERIMENT. Fill a large test tube with hydrogen. Keep the tube inverted until you can pick up a similar-sized tube in an inverted position. Turn the mouth of the gas-filled tube upward under the mouth of the inverted one—just as if you were pouring upward. To make the instructions as simple as possible, suppose we call the tube filled with hydrogen **A** and the air-filled, inverted container **B**. After holding the mouth of **A** upward under the mouth of **B** for 15 or 20 seconds, invert **A**. Keep **B** inverted also.

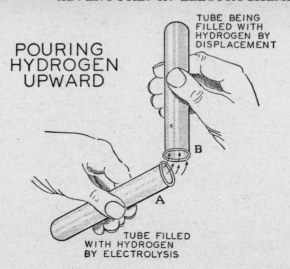

POURING
HYDROGEN
UPWARD

TUBE BEING
FILLED WITH
HYDROGEN BY
DISPLACEMENT

B

A

TUBE FILLED
WITH HYDROGEN
BY ELECTROLYSIS

Then test the contents of **A** with a lighted taper or splinter. Next test **B** in the same way. The contents of **A** will not burn. The contents of **B** will burn. The hydrogen was POURED UPWARD from **A** into **B**.

The Reducing Power of Hydrogen

Compounds of oxygen with one other element are called OXIDES. Hydrogen has the power to remove the oxygen from many oxides. Substances which have this power are called reducing agents. The process of combining with oxygen is called OXIDATION. Reduction is the reverse of oxidation.

Oxidation may also be defined as the loss of electrons, and reduction as the gain of electrons. Because of its ability to reduce metallic oxides to the free metal, hydrogen is used in metallurgical processes. The Brassert

Process uses hydrogen to reduce magnetite (an oxide of iron, Fe_3O_4) directly to a sponge iron without liquefying. Compressed sponge iron is used for making high-grade steels in the electric furnace. Tungsten, molybdenum, tantalum, and palladium are some of the metals obtained by reducing their oxides at high temperatures with hydrogen.

EXPERIMENTS WITH OXYGEN

Oxygen is the most abundant element on earth. It exists both free and combined. In the free state it makes up about one-fifth of the atmosphere by volume. Combined, which means compounded with other substances, it is by

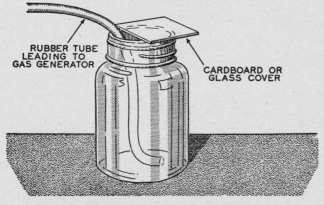

COLLECTING OXYGEN BY DOWNWARD DISPLACEMENT

RUBBER TUBE
LEADING TO
GAS GENERATOR

CARDBOARD OR
GLASS COVER

Oxygen's weight makes it possible to fill a jar by displacement. The oxygen is fed slowly into the jar at the bottom. The air in the jar is pushed upward and out by the incoming oxygen. Some air will be mixed with the oxygen, and the latter will not be as pure as it is when collected by the displacement of water.

weight nearly 50 per cent of all terrestrial matter and 89 per cent of water. Men and animals breathe it every minute of the day and night. If deprived of it for a few minutes, their life ceases. Plants also take in oxygen to a limited extent. All fuels require oxygen in order to burn.

A Test for Oxygen

EXPERIMENT. Fill a small jar with oxygen and remove it from the pneumatic trough. Thrust a glowing splinter into the jar. The wood will instantly burst into flame. Only two gases will bring about this result. One is oxygen and the other nitrous oxide. Nitrous oxide is a compound of oxygen with nitrogen.

When Carbon Burns in Oxygen, Carbon Dioxide Is Formed

Carbon dioxide is a colorless gas formed by the union of carbon and oxygen. There is a small amount in the atmosphere—in country air there is from 3 to 4 cubic feet of carbon dioxide in 10,000 cubic feet of atmosphere. In cities there is usually about twice as much carbon dioxide as in the country. Carbon dioxide is formed when carbon, or matter containing carbon, is burned. The same chemical process also occurs in the bodies of animals during respiration. The carbon dioxide found in the atmosphere comes from several sources, mainly combustion, respiration, fermentation, decay, and the decomposition of the mineral compounds called CARBONATES. Limestone, marble, and chalk are carbonates. "Soda water," root beer, "Coke," ginger ale, beer, champagne, and similar carbonated beverages contain carbon dioxide held in solution under slight pressure. When a bottle of carbonated beverage is opened, the pressure is released and the carbon dioxide is given opportunity to escape from the solution in the form of bubbles; we say the solution sparkles and effervesces. When sufficiently compressed, carbon dioxide becomes a liquid. About 1½ million tons of carbon dioxide are produced annually in the United States for use in beverages and in the manufacture of washing and baking sodas.

EXPERIMENT. Fill a 1-pint jar with oxygen and remove it from the pneumatic trough. Wind a wire about 10 inches long around a small piece of charcoal. The purpose of the wire is to serve as a sort of handle for the

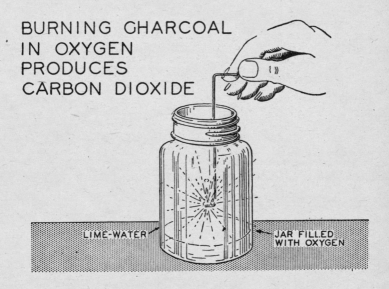

BURNING CHARCOAL IN OXYGEN PRODUCES CARBON DIOXIDE

LIME-WATER

JAR FILLED WITH OXYGEN

charcoal. Hold the charcoal in a gas flame, or in the flame of an alcohol lamp, until it ignites. Thrust the glowing charcoal into the jar of oxygen. Brilliant, rapid combustion will take place and continue until all the charcoal or all the oxygen is consumed. When the display is over, remove the charcoal and wire and cover the jar.

Charcoal is composed principally of carbon, and when it burns in oxygen it forms carbon dioxide. We can expect to find carbon dioxide in the jar. You can prove that the gas in the jar is carbon dioxide by pouring in a little clear limewater and shaking it. The limewater will become cloudy. When carbon dioxide mixes with limewater, the limewater becomes cloudy or milky as a result of the formation of chalk, which is calcium carbonate. Since no other gas has the same effect upon limewater,

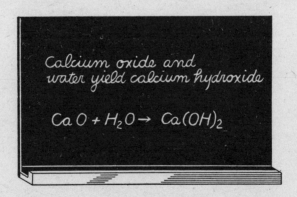

Calcium oxide and water yield calcium hydroxide

$$CaO + H_2O \rightarrow Ca(OH)_2$$

THE REACTION WHICH PRODUCES CALCIUM HYDROXIDE

Limewater is a solution of calcium hydroxide. It can be used to show the presence of carbon dioxide.

here is visible proof of the presence of a gas which is itself invisible.

To make limewater, drop a teaspoonful of hydrated or agricultural lime into a clean milk bottle nearly filled with clean water. Shake it thoroughly for two or three minutes. Then let it settle. Pour off some of the clear liquid at the top into another bottle and label it LIME-WATER. Keep it tightly corked until you are ready to use it.

SULFUR DIOXIDE

Sulfur dioxide is a colorless gas with a sharp, suffocating odor. It is evolved from active volcanoes and also occurs in very small quantities in the atmosphere. Immense quantities of sulfur dioxide are used in the manu-

Sulfur burns with a blue flame in oxygen and forms sulfur dioxide.

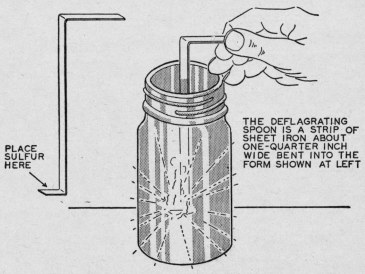

PLACE
SULFUR
HERE

THE DEFLAGRATING
SPOON IS A STRIP OF
SHEET IRON ABOUT
ONE-QUARTER INCH
WIDE BENT INTO THE
FORM SHOWN AT LEFT

facture of sulfuric acid and for bleaching. When sulfur burns in oxygen, it forms sulfur dioxide.

EXPERIMENT.   Make a "deflagrating spoon" by bending the ends of a narrow strip of sheet metal (about ⅜ inch wide and 8 inches long) cut from a tin can. See illustration. Place some powdered sulfur on the lower end of the spoon and ignite it with the flame of a match. The sulfur will melt first and then catch fire. As soon as it burns, thrust it into a pint jar which has been filled with oxygen. The sulfur will burn in the oxygen with a beautiful blue flame—much more brilliantly than it did in the air. The sharp odor you will probably notice is that of sulfur dioxide. Sulfur dioxide combines with water to form SULFUROUS ACID, a weak, unstable acid sometimes used as a bleach. Sulfurous acid forms BISULFITES and SULFITES with each metal or base. Calcium bisulfite is used in large quantities in the manufacture of paper. It has the ability to dissolve lignin, the substance that cements the fibers of cellulose in wood pulp.

Burning Iron

EXPERIMENT.   Heat a piece of iron wire bright red in the flame of a gas stove or Bunsen burner. Before it has a chance to cool, plunge the red-hot end into some powdered sulfur so that a small amount of sulfur adheres to the wire and takes fire. Plunge it quickly into a jar of oxygen. The iron will burn with beautiful scintillations. For a few seconds the burning sulfur will produce a blue flame. As soon as the sulfur is exhausted there will be no flame, but red-hot particles will be thrown off from the burning iron. The reddish-brown substance found in the jar after combustion has ceased is oxide of iron.

Making Ferric (Iron) Oxide by Electrolysis

Ferric oxide is a combination of iron and oxygen consisting of two atoms of iron combined with three atoms of oxygen. It is a brownish-red powder which is sold as "rouge"; "Indian," or "Persian," red; and "Venetian" red. Ferric oxide is used as a coloring pigment in paint and as a polishing powder for metal and glass. Persian red is a variety of ferric oxide used in cosmetic rouge and lipstick. Natural ferric oxide is found in abundance in nature as the ore HEMATITE.

IRON OXIDE BY ELECTROLYSIS

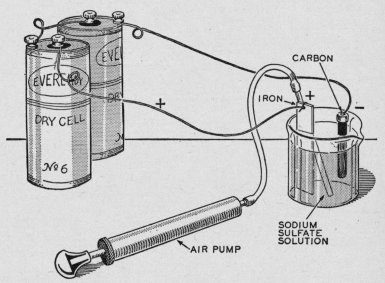

The sodium sulfate solution must be aerated by a stream of air bubbles which trickle up against the surfaces of the iron anode while the current is passing through the solution. The reddish-brown powder which forms is ferric oxide.

Ferrous oxide, consisting of one atom of iron and one atom of oxygen, is black and catches fire spontaneously in the air.

EXPERIMENT. Dissolve one level teaspoonful of sodium sulfate (Glauber's salts) in a pint jar nearly filled with lukewarm water. Connect a lead electrode about 4 inches $\times$ ½ inch to the negative terminal of three No. 6 dry cells in series and a 5 inch $\times$ ¾ inch strip of clean sheet iron to the positive terminal. Immerse the lead electrode and the iron electrode in the sodium sulfate solution.

The solution must be kept aerated by a stream of air bubbles which trickle upward against the sides of the iron anode while current is passing through the solution. The simplest method of supplying air is to use an aquarium pump. A tube connected to a small tire pump or to a small pump used for inflating footballs and basketballs can also be used.

In a few minutes, the electrolyte will assume a reddish-brown color which is due to a reddish-brown powder suspended in the solution. The powder can be obtained by filtering and drying. It is FERRIC OXIDE formed in the electrolyte by the union of ferric iron ions with oxygen ions.

NOTE. When mixing the electrolyte it is important not to add more than one level teaspoonful of powdered sodium sulfate to 16 fluid ounces of water (one pint). Sodium sulfate can be purchased at many drugstores. The druggist's (old-fashioned) name for sodium sulfate is Glauber's salts.

The Electrolysis of Magnesium Sulfate
Produces "Milk of Magnesia"

The chemist's name for "Milk of Magnesia," used as a medicine and in toothpaste, is MAGNESIUM HYDROXIDE. Commercial magnesium hydroxide is produced from magnesium compounds by purely chemical methods. It can be made by electrolysis, and the demonstration is an interesting experiment for the amateur electrochemist. EXPERIMENT. Dissolve 3 teaspoonfuls of magnesium sulfate (the druggist's name for this is Epsom salt) in an 8-ounce tumbler or beaker glass nearly filled with hot water. Set the solution over an alcohol lamp or a Bunsen burner turned down low. The solution should not boil but should be kept close to the boiling point. Connect two carbon rods from a size D dry cell to a battery composed of three No. 6 dry cells. Immerse the electrodes in the hot solution. As soon as current flows, a white precipitate will begin to form. This is the first time that the word "precipitate" has been used in this book. Perhaps it should be explained that a precipitate is a substance in a solid or condensed state separated from a solution in consequence of some chemical or physical change. The white precipitate formed in this experiment is MAGNESIUM HYDROXIDE. Magnesium hydroxide is only sparingly soluble in water. It has an alkaline reaction.

TWO KINDS OF COPPER IONS

The discovery and use of copper was one of the great milestones of man's cultural progress after the Stone

Age. With this metal and its natural alloys, he was able to make tools and other articles which could not be made from stone. Copper was obtained on the island of Cyprus by the Greeks and Romans. At first the red metal was called *cyprium,* but the name changed in the course of time to the Latin *cuprum.*

Copper is one of the metals which has two valences, or combining powers. It forms two series of salts: those called CUPROUS, in which the combining power of the copper atom equals that of an atom of hydrogen; and those called CUPRIC, in which the valence, or combining power, equals that of two atoms of hydrogen.

Copper, therefore, forms two kinds of ions. When cuprous salts are dissolved in water they form cuprous ions. The cupric salts form cupric ions. The cuprous ion is colorless, but the cupric ion is blue. Copper sulfate is a cupric salt of copper, and it is the cupric ion which gives a solution of copper sulfate its typical blue color. This can be shown by the electrolysis of a copper sulfate solution.

The Cupric Ion Is Blue

EXPERIMENT. Place a carbon rod from a size D flashlight cell inside a test tube from which the bottom has been cut off. Connect the carbon to the positive terminal of a battery of three No. 6 dry cells and immerse it and the tube in a solution of copper sulfate which has been slightly acidulated by the addition of one or two drops of dilute sulfuric acid. Arrange a strip of copper to encircle the test tube and connect it to the negative terminal of the battery. (See illustration.) A piece of stiff bare copper wire can be used in place of a copper strip.

Mix the electrolyte by dissolving 2 level teaspoonfuls of powdered copper sulfate in one pint of warm water and adding 5 drops of dilute sulfuric acid.

An electric current will flow between the carbon anode and the copper cathode. In a short time the solution near the copper cathode will be distinctly lighter in color. In a few minutes more it will have lost the blue color which is due to the presence of cupric ions. The cupric ions in the electrolyte close to the strip will have been attracted to the anode, lost their electric charge, and changed into copper atoms, and these atoms will leave the solution and plate out as spongy copper on the strip.

THE CUPRIC ION IS BLUE

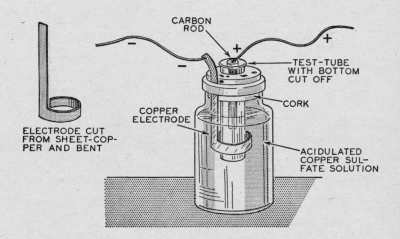

Chapter Twelve

Rectifiers

HOW ALTERNATING CURRENT CAN BE CHANGED TO DIRECT CURRENT · AN EXPERIMENTAL RECTIFIER · ELECTROLYTIC CAPACITORS · A HOMEMADE GALVANOSCOPE

The 120-volt current supplied by utility companies for household power is almost without exception alternating current and cannot be used for electrolytic experiments or for recharging storage batteries.

It is often desirable to convert small amounts of alternating current into direct current for use in radio and television circuits, electroplating, battery charging, and laboratory use. The process of changing alternating current to direct current is known as RECTIFICATION, and the device that accomplishes it is generally called a RECTIFIER.

It is possible to use an A.C. motor driving a D.C. generator for this purpose, but unless considerable power is required, a rectifier is more practical. The rectifier is simpler, more compact, and costs less.

Direct current is required in the plate circuits of all ordinary radio and television receivers. Electron valves, called vacuum tube rectifiers, are used for this purpose. Electron valves of a different type are used to some extent in automobile service stations to recharge storage batteries. The type used for storage-battery recharging, technically called a "hot-cathode gas-filled rectifier tube," is also known under the trade-names, "Tungar Bulb" and "Rectigon Bulb." Inside the glass envelope is a tungsten filament which forms the cathode, and directly above it is an anode in the form of a disk of graphite. The envelope is filled with rarefied argon gas. When

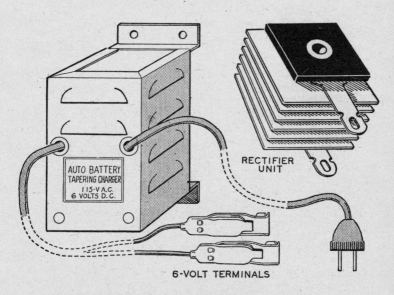

AUTO BATTERY
TAPERING CHARGER
115-V A.C.
6 VOLTS D.C.

RECTIFIER
UNIT

6-VOLT TERMINALS

SMALL RECTIFIER FOR CHARGING AUTOMOBILE STORAGE BATTERIES

the filament is red-hot, the device becomes an electrical valve. Current between the filament and the electrode will pass in one direction only. One-half of each cycle of an alternating current can pass, but not the other half. If placed in an alternating current circuit, the tube will rectify alternating current into a pulsating direct current.

A type of rectifier in common use in small battery chargers, in radio and television receivers, and in laboratories utilizes a peculiar characteristic of certain materials; this characteristic is called SEMI-CONDUCTION.

In addition to conductors and non-conductors of electric current, there are materials called SEMI-CONDUCTORS. A semi-conductor is neither a good conductor like metallic silver or copper, nor a non-conductor like glass. One of the useful properties of a semi-conductor is its ability to permit the flow of electricity in one direction and to resist its flow in the opposite direction. It acts as an automatic electrical valve, opening to electrons passing in one direction and closing to those which try to move the opposite way. Germanium, selenium, silicon, copper sulfide, and copper oxide are the semi-conductors most used in rectifiers in the electrical and electronic fields.

Silicon, selenium, and magnesium-copper sulfide rectifiers in a great variety of sizes and types are of increasing industrial importance because of their versatility. The rectifying disks of silicon, selenium, or magnesium-copper sulfide and the metal plates between them are firmly bolted together in a bank, or group. Metallic fins, or plates, are placed alongside each rectifying disk to dissipate the heat produced by the passage of current.

ELECTROLYTIC RECTIFIERS

Several varieties of rectifier which employ electrolysis in their operation have been devised and placed on the market, but none of them have proved to be practical from a commercial standpoint. During the first decade of this century, aluminum electrolytic rectifiers were manufactured. Aluminum can acquire a thin coating of aluminum oxide very quickly. When an aluminum electrode is immersed in an electrolyte, it will become covered with a layer of oxide almost instantly if used as the anode in an electric circuit. Aluminum oxide is an insulator, and the oxide coating on the electrode will interrupt the current flow. If the aluminum electrode is then made the cathode in the circuit, the aluminum oxide is reduced and disappears almost instantly.

Aluminum electrolytic rectifiers utilize the almost instantaneous oxidation and reduction which occurs on an aluminum electrode to change alternating current into direct current. This same property of aluminum is also used in the manufacture of electrolytic capacitors, one of the common components of radio receivers.

Aluminum electrolytic rectifiers will handle only small amounts of current. They are not an efficient means of rectifying alternating current. The liquid electrolyte makes them non-portable. They are no longer manufactured commercially.

ELECTROLYTIC CAPACITORS

The fact that a non-conducting layer of aluminum oxide forms quickly on the surface of aluminum is utilized in the construction of electrolytic CAPACITORS. It would be difficult to find an electronic circuit in which there is not at least one capacitor. There are several capacitors in the common home broadcast receiver and usually at least one electrolytic capacitor among them.

What is a Capacitor?

Capacitors were formerly called electric condensers. The correct name is now "capacitor." A capacitor consists of two conducting metal plates separated by a layer of insulating material known as the DIELECTRIC. The plates are usually sheet aluminum or aluminum foil. The common dielectrics used in capacitors are air, mica, paper, oil, and a thin layer of aluminum oxide. Capacitors using an aluminum oxide dielectric are electrolytic capacitors.

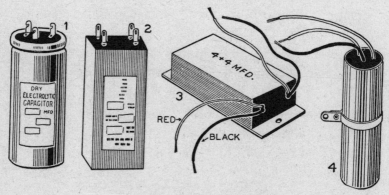

ELECTROLYTIC CAPACITORS

The almost instantaneous formation of an insulating coating of aluminum oxide on an aluminum anode is utilized in building electrolytic capacitors which provide large capacitance in small space. Capacitors of this type are widely used in radio and motor-starting circuits.

Electrolytic capacitors may be either wet or "dry." Both types are actually wet inside, but the so-called "dry" type contains no free liquid, whereas the wet type does. The wet type of capacitor consists of sheets of aluminum foil immersed in a solution of borax in water. The borax solution, since it is an electrolyte, serves as one of the conducting surfaces in the capacitor. Electrolytic action is used to form a thin coat of aluminum oxide on the surface of the aluminum foil. The aluminum oxide serves as the insulating dielectric between the aluminum foil and the electrolyte. Wet-type electrolytic capacitors are usually enclosed in an aluminum can.

The "dry" type of electrolytic capacitor also consists of aluminum foil and a solution of borax. However, the electrolyte is contained in wet gauze or paper or is in a thick jelly so that there is no free liquid.

Electrolytic capacitors are always marked to indicate the positive and negative terminals.

An electrolytic capacitor can be manufactured at much lower cost than capacitors of equal capacitance of other types. Also they are smaller in physical dimensions. Because of their small size and low cost, electrolytic capacitors are commonly used in the power supply circuits of broadcast receivers. They are also used in the motor-starting circuits of oil-burners, air-conditioners, and electric refrigerators. The aluminum oxide film between the aluminum foil and the electrolyte deteriorates with age. Consequently, a breakdown of an electrolytic capacitor is one of the most frequent causes of receiver failure, a difficulty which is quickly overcome by the installation of a new capacitor.

CAUTION. The following experiment and those with the electrolytic rectifier which follow in this chapter require the use of the 120-volt house-lighting current. They are intended only for science teachers and older students to demonstrate—students who are able to handle the apparatus with intelligence and care. If two electrodes are touched at the same time when the apparatus is connected to the household current, they may give a shock —not a severe shock, of course, because there is a lamp in circuit. It is not advisable to use any electrical apparatus connected to the 120-volt current in a room with a concrete floor. The apparatus should not be plugged into an outlet until ready for use. As soon as the experiments are completed, disconnect the apparatus by pulling the plug out of the socket.

An Experiment Which Demonstrates the Formation of a Film of Aluminum Oxide and Its Insulating Quality on an Aluminum Anode

The lead plates, the aluminum plates, the wood pieces, lamp socket, fruit jars, and electrolyte used in this experiment can be utilized also to make an electrolytic rectifier.
EXPERIMENT. Make two wood pieces 3½ inches × 1⅛ inches × ¾ inch, and give each of them two coats of shellac or paint them with hot paraffin to prevent the wood from absorbing electrolyte.

Cut four electrodes 7½ inches × 1¼ inches from sheet aluminum and two of the same size from sheet lead. The illustration shows the location of two small holes which should be drilled in each electrode. The hole nearest the end is for the screw which holds a binding post, or connector, to each electrode. The other hole is for the round-head wood screw which holds the electrode to the wood support.

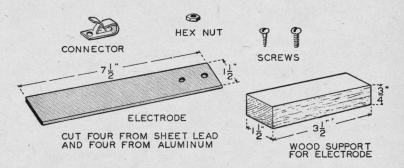

HEX NUT

SCREWS

CONNECTOR

7½"

1½"

ELECTRODE

CUT FOUR FROM SHEET LEAD
AND FOUR FROM ALUMINUM

3¾"

½"   3½"

WOOD SUPPORT
FOR ELECTRODE

PARTS FOR THE RECTIFIER

Two 1-quart fruit jars are used as containers for the electrolyte. Fill them with warm water to about 1¼ inches from the top. Add 3 level tablespoonfuls of borax to the water in each jar and stir until dissolved.

Use ⅜-inch round-head wood screws to attach one aluminum electrode and one lead electrode to opposite sides of each wood strip. Hang each set of electrodes in a jar of borax solution. Connect the two cells in series and in series with a 75-watt, 120-volt incandescent lamp connected to the 120-volt A.C. lighting circuit.

Notice that the 75-watt lamp does not light to full brilliance. It gives a reddish glow instead of a white light. The lamp does not get sufficient voltage and amperage to light to full brilliance, because 60 times per second (once each cycle) the aluminum plates are positive, in other words they are anodes, and a film of aluminum oxide forms on them and cuts off the current. Only one-half of each alternating current cycle passes through the cells and lamp. The current can flow only when the aluminum electrodes are negative and the aluminum oxide is reduced.

Shut off the current and remove both sets of plates from the electrolyte. Take off the lead plates and replace them with aluminum plates, so that each wood strip has two aluminum strips mounted on it at opposite sides. Save the lead plates for making a rectifier. Immerse both sets of aluminum plates in the electrolyte. Connect them in series and also in series with the 75-watt lamp and 120-volt alternating current supply. The lamp WILL NOT

DEMONSTRATION OF THE FORMATION OF ALUMINUM OXIDE AND ITS INSULATING QUALITY

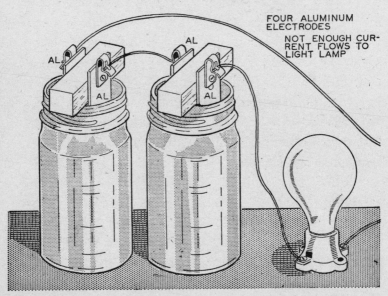

FOUR ALUMINUM ELECTRODES

NOT ENOUGH CURRENT FLOWS TO LIGHT LAMP

AL

AL

AL

AL

LIGHT. In this arrangement there is always an aluminum electrode in each cell which is positive and is therefore covered with an insulating film of aluminum oxide which effectively blocks passage of all but a very small amount of current, not enough to light the lamp.

How Electrolysis Can Rectify an Alternating Current

The amateur electrochemist can make an experimental electrolytic rectifier and demonstrate that alternating current can be converted into direct current by electrolytic action.

An electrolytic rectifier consists of two electrodes, one of which must be aluminum, immersed in an electrolyte. The aluminum electrode, the electrolyte, and the electric current do the actual rectifying. The other electrode, which may be carbon or lead, does not take any active part in the rectifying action except to make contact with the electrolyte. The electrolyte may be a solution of sodium phosphate or of household borax. Borax is an inexpensive and satisfactory electrolyte for an experimental rectifier.

The action of the aluminum electrode in changing alternating current into direct current is that of an electrical valve which opens to the flow of current in one direction and closes when the current flows in the opposite direction.

An electrolytic rectifier may consist of more than one cell, but in order to understand the rectifying process let us consider a single cell consisting of an aluminum plate and a lead plate immersed in a borax solution. If the positive pole of a battery is connected to the lead electrode and the negative pole to the aluminum electrode, the current from the battery will flow through the rectifier and continue to do so until the battery is exhausted or the current is shut off. Nothing unusual will happen. A small amount of gas will be released at the lead and aluminum plates and that is all.

However, if the poles of the battery are reversed so that the positive pole is connected to the aluminum electrode, the current will flow for an infinitesimal fraction of a second only, and then it will cease. The reason for this is that when the aluminum electrode is positive, oxygen forms on its surface and a thin coating of aluminum oxide forms on the electrode wherever it is in contact with the electrolyte. Since aluminum oxide is an insulator, it shields the aluminum electrode from the electrolyte sufficiently to prevent the passage of a low-voltage current.

If the battery poles are reversed so that the aluminum electrode is negative, hydrogen forms on the aluminum and REDUCES the aluminum oxide to aluminum. With the disappearance of the oxide, the aluminum electrode is again in contact with the electrolyte and current can flow.

The formation and reduction of the aluminum oxide are almost instantaneous, in fact so rapid that if a low-voltage, 60-cycle alternating current (reversing 120 times per second) is passed through an electrolytic rectifier, the "valve" action occurs 60 times per second and permits the current to flow freely in one direction but not in the other.

The current which passes is principally an intermittent direct current, that is, it flows in one direction. The nature of the current will depend to some extent upon the voltage applied to the rectifier terminals. The "electrical valve" will "leak" if the voltage is too high. In that case there will be strong pulses of current in one direction and weak pulses in the opposite direction.

How to Make an Experimental Electrolytic Rectifier

EXPERIMENT. Make two wood pieces 3½ inches × 1⅛ inches × ¾ inch and give each of them two coats of shellac or paint them with hot paraffin. Either of these protective coatings will prevent the wood from absorbing any of the electrolyte and becoming conductive. The electrodes are supported by these pieces, and if the wood absorbs any electrolyte it will provide an undesirable current leak between the electrodes.

Cut two electrodes 7½ inches × 1¼ inches from sheet aluminum and two of the same size from sheet lead. The illustration shows the location of two holes which should be drilled in each electrode. The hole nearest the end is for attaching a binding post, or connector, to each electrode. The other hole is for the screw which holds the electrode to the wood support.

Two 1-quart fruit jars are used as containers for the electrolyte. Fill them with warm water to about 1¼ inches from the top. Add 3 level tablespoonfuls of borax to the water in each jar and stir until dissolved.

One limitation of an electrolytic rectifier is its low current-carrying capacity. Another is that it is only efficient on low voltages. When used to rectify 120-volt alternating current, the two rectifier cells should be connected in series with a 120-volt incandescent lamp. The resistance of the lamp will lower both the voltage and amperage of the A.C. current applied to the rectifier terminals. The lamp should be placed in a porcelain base socket mounted on a wood base, so that the hot glass envelope of the lamp cannot touch nearby objects and scorch them.

The aluminum electrode is the positive terminal of the rectifier. The lead is the negative terminal.

The illustration shows the two-cell rectifier just de-

TWO-CELL EXPERIMENTAL ELECTROLYTIC RECTIFIER

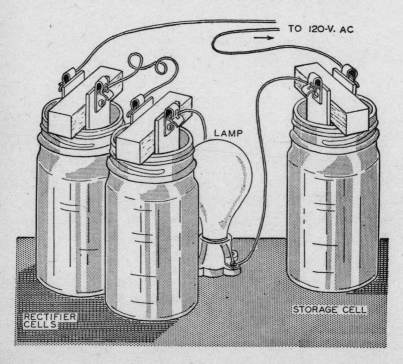

scribed connected to a 2-volt storage cell. If you have a 6-volt storage battery in your laboratory, it can be kept charged by this "trickle" charger. The rectifier is connected to the battery whenever the latter is not in use, so that a small amount of rectified current "trickles" into the battery and recharges it. If the lamp connected in series with the rectifier and battery is a 120-volt, 150-watt lamp, about ½ ampere will trickle into the battery. Do not use a larger lamp. It will pass too much current for the rectifier to handle without overheating.

NOTE: The positive pole of the battery must be connected only to the aluminum electrode, or positive pole, of the rectifier.

When the rectifier is in operation, a direct current ammeter with a low reading scale (0-2 amps or 0-5 amps) connected in series with the battery will indicate a direct current of 0.4 to 0.6 amps. If the current were not direct current, the meter would not indicate; the needle would flutter near the zero mark.

If a suitable ammeter is not available, you can use a homemade galvanoscope. A galvanoscope will detect feeble currents of electricity. When connected to a source of direct current, the needle of the galvanoscope will swing to the right or to the left, depending upon which way the current flows through the galvanoscope coils. If the galvanoscope is connected to a circuit in which a 60-cycle A.C. current is flowing, the needle will not assume any definite right- or left-hand position but will merely vibrate. There are instructions for building a galvanoscope at the end of this chapter.

A FOUR-CELL ELECTROLYTIC RECTIFIER

Two rectifier cells connected in series with a lamp and battery will rectify only one-half of each alternating cycle. When four cells are used, both halves of the alternating current cycle are rectified. The method of connecting four rectifier cells in order to secure this result is illustrated. The lamp bank, placed in series with the A.C. current source, should consist of two 75-watt, 120-volt lamps or one 150-watt, 120-volt lamp. If a single 75-watt lamp is used, the rectifier will produce a direct current current of about ½ ampere. If two 75-watt lamps or a single 150-watt lamp is used, the direct current will be about 1 ampere. Do not use more lamps or lamps of greater wattage than specified or the rectifier cells will overheat and not operate long.

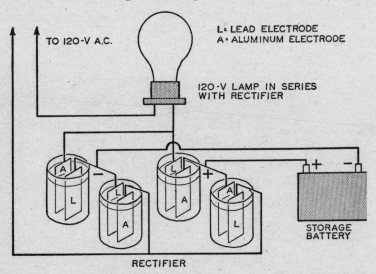

TO 120-V A.C.

L: LEAD ELECTRODE
A: ALUMINUM ELECTRODE

120-V LAMP IN SERIES
WITH RECTIFIER

+ −

STORAGE
BATTERY

RECTIFIER

CIRCUIT DIAGRAM OF A FOUR-CELL ELECTROLYTIC RECTIFIER

The borax solution in rectifier cells of approximately 1-quart capacity will become exhausted after about twenty to twenty-four hours of operation in delivering current at ½ ampere. Before it is exhausted it should be replaced with fresh electrolyte. One of the first indications that the electrolyte is exhausted is its becoming very hot. The lead electrodes will last a long time. The life of the aluminum electrodes will depend upon the thickness of the material from which they are cut and upon the alloy from which they are made. Ordinary aluminum sheet is not pure aluminum but is an alloy of aluminum with other metals.

How to Make a Galvanoscope

Wind about 40 turns of small insulated copper magnet wire around a 6-ounce jelly glass near the bottom of the glass. The wires should be bunched closely together. Use any size of magnet wire from No. 25 B. S. to No. 34 B. S. This will form a coil with an inside diameter of about 2 inches. A jelly glass is used because it is tapered and the coil can easily be slipped off. The terminals (ends of the wire) of the coil should be about 3 inches long. Slip the coil off the jelly glass carefully and bind it at three or four points with thread or Scotch tape so that the wire turns are held closely together. Mark the inside, or beginning, end and the outside, or finishing, end of the wire so that you can identify them and tell which is which. Make two coils exactly alike in this way. Wind both coils in the same direction.

Fasten the two coils about 1½ inches apart to a 4

inch × 3½ inch × ¾ inch wood base with sealing wax as shown in the illustration. Mount two binding posts, or connectors, on the wood base. Connect the inside terminal of coil No. 1 to one of the binding posts. Connect the outside terminal of coil No. 1 to the inside terminal of coil No. 2. Connect the outside terminal of coil No. 2 to the second binding post.

The needle for the galvanoscope is a large sewing needle which has been magnetized by rubbing the point on one of the poles of a permanent magnet. The needle should be mounted in a little strip of thick writing paper

HOMEMADE GALVANOSCOPE

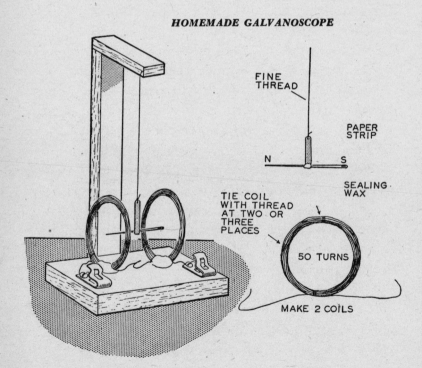

FINE THREAD

PAPER STRIP

N   S

SEALING WAX

TIE COIL WITH THREAD AT TWO OR THREE PLACES

50 TURNS

MAKE 2 COILS

or drawing paper. Find the place at which the needle will balance in the paper strip and fasten it there with a small drop of Duco cement or molten sealing wax. Use a pin to punch a hole in the other end of the paper strip and tie a fine silk thread through it. The other end of the thread is supported by two wood strips fastened together in the shape of the letter "L" and attached to the rear edge of the base. The thread should be attached to the over-hanging support so that the needle hangs in the center of the space between the two coils. The needle should be free to swing horizontally without touching either coil.

If you do not have a strong permanent magnet for magnetizing the needle, wrap 25 or 30 turns of small insulated magnet wire around the needle and connect the terminals to a 1½-volt dry cell. Allow the current to flow for ten or fifteen seconds; then disconnect the wire and unwind it from the needle.

When the magnetized needle hangs from the silk thread, it will act as a compass needle and point in a north and south direction.

When the galvanoscope is used, it is necessary to turn it around until the coils are parallel to the needle after the latter has come to rest in a north and south position. Then, if a very feeble electric current flows through the coils, the needle will swing around in line with the axis of the coils.

The galvanoscope was much used by the first electrical scientists. It was eventually developed into an instrument called a galvanometer and finally into the measuring instruments called ammeters and voltmeters.

ANODIZED ALUMINUM

Corrosion is a major problem in the use of aluminum for marine construction, especially for naval aircraft. The fact that a heavy coat of aluminum oxide will form on aluminum when it is made the anode in an electrolytic cell provides an inexpensive method of protecting aluminum surfaces from corrosion. ANODIZED aluminum has remarkable corrosion-resistance properties.

Chapter Thirteen

Electroplating—
Electrotyping—Electroforming

Many metals are successfully plated in thin, firmly adherent sheets on other metals by electrolysis. These include silver, gold, copper, nickel, zinc, chromium, cadmium, and several others. The process is called ELECTROPLATING. There is little commercial use of any metals for electroplating except those just mentioned. The purpose of electroplating is generally to improve resistance to corrosion or to enhance the appearance of a metal surface. For example, sheet iron used in the manufacture of food cans and other containers is plated with tin to protect it from rust and corrosion. Low-priced brooches, charms, bracelets, and costume jewelry made of inexpensive base metals are gold-plated to impart the appearance of gold.

Objects made of wax, plaster, wood and other non-conducting materials can be electroplated by first giving them a conducting surface. This is done usually by brushing them with finely powdered graphite. (Graphite is a form of carbon.) Contact is made with the graphited surface by a fine copper wire.

ELECTROPLATING A CARBON ROD

Although carbon is not a metal, it is a good conductor of electric current and is easily electroplated. If two flashlight cell carbons are connected to the terminals of a 3-volt battery and immersed in a solution of copper sulfate, the carbon rod connected to the negative terminal of the battery will become plated with copper. Part of the copper sulfate dissociates when it goes into solution and forms positively charged copper ions and negatively charged sulfate ions. The positive copper ions are attracted to the negative carbon rod. There they are relieved of their charge and become copper atoms which adhere to the carbon rod.

The graphite blocks and rods used as brushes in motors and generators are usually electroplated with copper so that they will make better electrical contact with their metal fixtures or holders.

EXPERIMENT. Connect two flashlight cell carbons to two dry cells connected in series, or to a 2-volt storage cell. Immerse the carbons in a tumbler or beaker glass filled with copper sulfate solution. Almost immediately a thin film of copper will appear on the carbon rod connected to the negative battery terminal. In time the plating will build up to a considerable thickness.

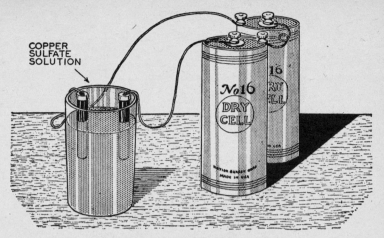

COPPER
SULFATE
SOLUTION

ELECTROPLATING A CARBON ROD

COPPER-PLATING A PIECE OF PAPER

EXPERIMENT. You can copper-plate a piece of paper, leather, or closely woven fine cloth. The procedure is the same in each instance. To plate a piece of paper, make both sides of a small strip of stiff paper conductive to an electric current by rubbing them thoroughly with powdered graphite. Use a wad of cotton or cotton cloth to apply and rub the graphite. Avoid touching the conducting surface with the fingers. Fold one end of the paper strip around the end of a bare copper wire so that the graphited surface makes electrical contact with the wire. Clamp the paper against the wire with a paper clip. Use a strip of sheet copper about 1 inch wide, connected to the positive terminal of two dry cells connected in series. Connect the wire attached to the graphite-covered paper strip to the negative terminal of the battery and immerse it in the copper sulfate solution. The paper strip acts as the cathode, and the black graphited surface immersed in the electrolyte will be covered gradually with a red layer of copper.

NICKEL-PLATING

It is quite easy to plate iron, steel, and brass with either nickel or copper. An important part of the process is preparing the article for plating. It must have a clean surface free from all rust, scale, dirt, and grease. Polishing on a buffing wheel is usually the first step. Rinsing in a weak solution of lye is the second step. The lye solution will remove all grease. It will be more effective if hot. Before plating, all traces of lye must be removed by rinsing in hot water.

The nickel-plating process is similar to copper-plating except that the electrolyte consists of 3 ounces of nickel ammonium sulfate dissolved in 1 quart of water and a pure nickel anode is used in place of a copper anode.

If the amateur electrochemist wishes to try his hand at nickel-plating, the work to be plated should be connected, after having been cleaned, to the negative terminal of a 2-volt storage cell. The nickel anode should be connected to the positive terminal of the storage cell.

When it comes from a plating bath, a nickeled object is dull. It must be buffed to give it the high polish characteristic of nickel. For best results, iron and steel articles are copper-plated before being nickeled.

One of the tricks of the electroplater's art is to regulate the amount of current which flows through the electrolyte so that a smooth, firm coating is built up upon the object being plated.

Chapter Fourteen

What Is Photoelectricity?

PHOTOELECTRIC CELLS AND PHOTOTUBES •

PHOTOELECTRIC EMISSION • AN EXPERIMENTAL

PHOTOELECTRIC CELL

Several chemicals, principally cuprous oxide, selenium, thorium, titanium, and the metals of the ALKALI group (lithium, sodium, potassium, rubidium, cesium, and francium) have PHOTOELECTRIC properties. They show electrical activity when exposed to light. There is a disturbance of the electrons in these photoelectric substances whenever they are struck by light. Some of them produce a feeble electric current under the influence of light. Photoelectric substances are used in making PHOTOCELLS or PHOTOELECTRIC cells, popularly called "electric eyes." Photocells and photoelectric cells are the correct names.

The exposure meters used in photography to measure the intensity of light consist of a photoelectric cell con-

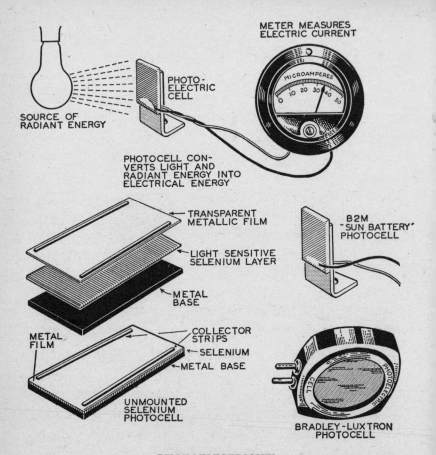

SOURCE OF
RADIANT ENERGY

PHOTO-
ELECTRIC
CELL

METER MEASURES
ELECTRIC CURRENT

MICROAMPERES

0 10 20 30 40 50

PHOTOCELL CON-
VERTS LIGHT AND
RADIANT ENERGY INTO
ELECTRICAL ENERGY

← TRANSPARENT
   METALLIC FILM

← LIGHT SENSITIVE
   SELENIUM LAYER

← METAL
   BASE

B 2 M
"SUN BATTERY"
PHOTOCELL

METAL
FILM

COLLECTOR
STRIPS

← SELENIUM

← METAL BASE

UNMOUNTED
SELENIUM
PHOTOCELL

BRADLEY-LUXTRON
PHOTOCELL

PHOTOELECTRICITY

Many photocells employ a thin layer of selenium. This substance generates an electric current when exposed to light.

nected to a sensitive meter which measures the electric current generated by the cell but is marked with graduations to indicate the correct exposure under existing light conditions.

Photoelectric cells are more sensitive to small changes in light intensity and color than human eyes. They have important uses other than as exposure meters. A photocell is used in every sound motion picture projector to detect and translate the fluctuating light produced by the sound track into current which will produce sounds from a loudspeaker when amplified. Photoelectric cells are used also to detect the presence of intruders; to operate counting machines; to open and close doors automatically; to keep color printing presses in "register," or adjustment; to dim automobile headlights when another car approaches; to inspect manufactured articles; to send photos and drawings by wire or radio; in fact, to do many things which seem almost like magic.

The Direct Conversion of the Energy of Light Into Electrical Energy

Alexander Graham Bell was the first to make a useful photocell. He made a selenium photocell in 1877. For many years it was thought to be only a current-conducting device whose resistance changed when it was exposed to light. At that time it was not known that a selenium cell could also be a photoelectric cell and that, in addition to changing its resistance, it could also generate an electromotive force which would move electrons when it was exposed to light. It is the photoelectric voltage-generating quality of selenium that is now most widely used.

The typical selenium photoelectric cell consists of a metal plate (usually iron), one side of which is covered with a layer of selenium. A thin film of gold or silver is spattered on the exposed surface of the selenium. A metal current-conducting electrode, or collector strip, rests on the gold or silver film near its edges and makes electrical contact with it. The gold or silver film is so extremely thin that it is semi-transparent and permits light to pass and reach the selenium layer underneath. When light shines on the cell, electrons move out of the selenium into the iron plate. If a wire is connected to the iron plate and to the collector strip so as to form a circuit, a small current will flow through the circuit. Under proper conditions the flow of current varies almost directly as the amount of light which reaches the selenium.

PHOTOTUBES

Not all photocells are constructed like a selenium cell and not all generate their own electromotive force. One different and widely used type is called a PHOTOTUBE and has the general appearance of the familiar radio tube used in radio receivers and amplifiers. The phototube consists principally of two electrodes sealed in a base like the base of a radio tube. The electrode in the center of the envelope is the cathode. It is a strip of thin, silver-plated sheet copper bent into semi-cylindrical form and connected to a prong on the base of the tube. The silver on the concave surface of the cathode is covered with a thin layer of cesium oxide, and the cesium oxide in turn is coated with a thin layer of metallic cesium. The anode of the tube is a short, straight rod or wire also connected to a prong on the base. When the phototube is in operation, the anode is connected to the positive terminal of a source of voltage.

The sensitized inner surface of the cathode is the only part of the phototube which is sensitive to light. The cathode becomes a source of electrons when its sensitized surface is exposed to light. Since electrons are negative and are attracted by a positive charge, they are attracted to the positive anode. They travel across the space between the cathode and anode and continue to do so as

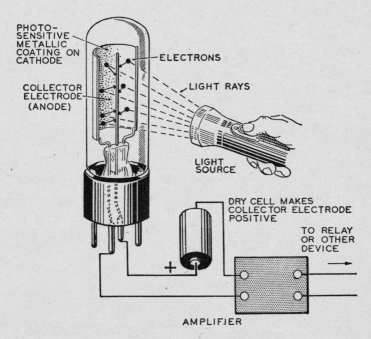

PHOTOELECTRICITY

A phototube type of photoelectric cell is illustrated. The current generated by photocells is very small and must be amplified before it is powerful enough to operate a relay, loudspeaker, etc.

long as radiant energy strikes the cathode and the anode remains positive. This movement of electrons is an electric current, and if the phototube is included in an electrical circuit, light can be used to control the strength of the current flowing in the circuit. The current is too weak (it is only a few millionths of an ampere) to operate any but the most sensitive relay. Therefore the current produced in a phototube by light rays is of necessity augmented by an electronic amplifier in many applications.

Cesium is not the only metal used in sensitizing the cathode in phototubes. Calcium, barium, and strontium and their oxides are used for this purpose. Tantalum, thorium, and titanium are utilized on the cathodes of special-purpose phototubes which respond to ultraviolet light but which are not sensitive to light in that portion of the spectrum which is visible to the human eye.

How to Make an Experimental Cuprous Oxide Photoelectric Cell

There are two oxides of copper, a black variety called CUPRIC oxide (CuO), and a red oxide called CUPROUS oxide (Cu_2O). Cupric oxide is the black coating which forms on the surface of copper when it is heated in the air. Hot cupric oxide is an active oxidizing agent, often used by chemists in the analysis of organic compounds.

Cuprous oxide has photoelectric properties and also rectifying action. The construction of a simple form of cuprous oxide photoelectric cell is an interesting experiment.

The first problem is how to make electrical contact with the exposed surface of the cuprous oxide. There is no easy way for the amateur electrochemist to spray an extremely thin transparent metallic coating on the oxide. It is easier to establish contact by means of a liquid electrolyte. When finished, the photoelectric cell will resemble a small homemade voltaic cell in appearance. The electrodes are a copper plate covered with cuprous oxide and a lead plate immersed in a solution of sodium chloride.

The current produced by photoelectric cells is extremely small. Commercial types of selenium photocells

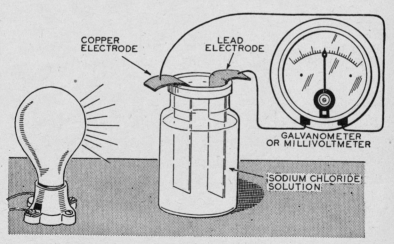

PHOTOELECTRIC CELL

COPPER ELECTRODE

LEAD ELECTRODE

GALVANOMETER OR MILLIVOLTMETER

SODIUM CHLORIDE SOLUTION

AN EXPERIMENTAL CUPROUS OXIDE PHOTOELECTRIC CELL

will produce only about eight milliamperes (.008 amps) for each square inch of active cell area exposed to average sunlight. In the homemade photocell described here, there are about 5 square inches of active cuprous oxide surface in contact with the electrolyte. This area will produce only about ½ milliampere when exposed to the light of a 150-watt lamp a few inches from the cell. To demonstrate that the cell converts light energy into electrical energy, it is necessary to connect it to a sensitive milliammeter with a scale reading 0 to 1 milliampere or 0 to 10 milliamperes. Meters of this type are probably not available to many amateur experimenters. High school physics laboratories often have this equipment. When a suitable meter is available, the homemade photocell is a good experiment for a science teacher to demonstrate to a class. A photocell displays the action called PHOTOELECTRIC EMISSION.

Explanation of Photoelectric Emission

There are electrons present within a metal which are free to move about within the interior of the metal. They are referred to as "free" electrons. It is the presence of these free electrons which makes metal an electrical conductor. The motions of free electrons are governed by some interesting basic laws. Normally the free electrons do not escape from the metal, because they do not have enough energy to overcome a potential barrier which exists at the surface of the metal. However, electrons may in several ways acquire sufficient energy to pass through the potential barrier and pass through a metal surface. One source of this additional energy is heat. It is heat which provides electrons with sufficient energy to escape from the hot cathode of a vacuum tube. Electromagnetic radiation of suitable wave length is another source from which the free electrons in a metal may obtain enough energy to pass through the surface barrier and escape. When a photon strikes the surface of a metal, a portion of all of the photon's energy may be imparted to an electron, enabling the electron to escape. "Photon" is the name used in the quantum theory for the elemental unit of energy. Light is electromagnetic radiation. The radiation which produces photoelectric emission includes the visible spectrum, ultraviolet light, and x-rays.

The Parts and Materials for the Photocell

Cut a lead electrode 4¼ inches long and 1 inch wide from sheet lead. Make a small hole (use a No. 29 or 30 drill) ⅝ inch from one end of the electrode. Rub both sides and the edges with sandpaper until all surfaces are bright and shining.

Cut a copper electrode the same size as the lead electrode from soft sheet copper (electrolytic). Drill a small hole in it ⅝ inch from one end and rub all surfaces with fine sandpaper until they are clean and bright.

Make a wood strip 3½ inches × 1⅛ inches × ¾ inch and give it two coats of white shellac. The electrodes are supported by this strip. They are held in place by two ⅜-inch round-head brass screws. The lead electrode can be mounted as soon as the shellac is dry, but the copper

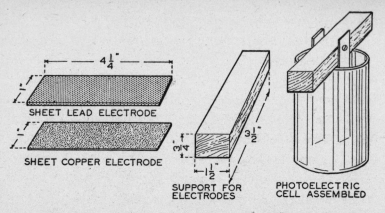

PARTS FOR THE EXPERIMENTAL PHOTOELECTRIC CELL

electrode is not put in place until it has been coated with cuprous oxide.

The electrolyte for the photocell is a solution of sodium chloride. Dissolve 3 level teaspoonfuls of table salt in 5 ounces of lukewarm water. Pour enough electrolyte into a straight-side 8-ounce glass tumbler to make the depth of the solution about 2½ inches. Prepare the electrolyte an hour before it will be needed, so that it can stand and clear.

Sensitizing the Copper Electrode

The success of the photocell depends to a large extent upon the copper electrode's being made photosensitive with a coating of cuprous oxide. If enough copper is available, it is advisable to make three or four electrodes and use the one which proves to be best. The oxide is formed by heating the electrode over a gas flame, preferably the flame of a gas stove, so that the entire electrode can be held close to the flame at the same time.

Have a 2-quart pan filled with cold water near. Grasp an upper corner of the electrode with a pair of pliers and hold it over a lighted burner close to the flame. Turn it over every 3 or 4 seconds. The surface of the copper will display iridescent colors which become red and finally black. When the surface on both sides of the electrode is colored evenly "light" black (if heated too long it will be "dark" black), withdraw the electrode from the heat and, after waiting about 5 seconds, drop it into the pan of cold water.

Here is what happens: If the copper is clean and has been brightened by rubbing with No. 000 sandpaper, it will become covered with a layer of red cuprous oxide. The outer surface of the cuprous oxide will change almost immediately to cupric oxide. This black, non-transparent material will shield the photosensitive cuprous oxide underneath from light, and in that condition the electrode is useless. However, if the black oxide is not allowed to become too black and too thick, it will be removed when the hot electrode is plunged into cold water. When the electrode is removed from the water, it will be a dull, dark red color and will be photosensitive. Note that both oxides will decompose into oxygen and metallic copper when heated to high temperatures.

EXPERIMENT. Fasten the copper electrode to the wood support on the side opposite the lead electrode. Make connection to each electrode with a piece of copper wire (each piece about 12 inches long) clamped under the screw or between the electrode and the wood strip. The copper electrode is the anode (positive), and the lead electrode is the cathode (negative). Connect the cell to a milliammeter. The anode must be connected to the terminal on the meter marked PLUS or with a + sign. The photocell has an electromotive force of approximately 0.5 volt and produces a current of approximately .002 to .0025 milliampere in the dark. If a 150-watt lamp is brought close to the cell, the voltage will not increase much but the current output may go up to .005 milliampere. Turning the light on and off and watching the meter reading will demonstrate the fact that light gives electrons the energy to move.

In some instances the current output of the photocell may exceed the maximum reading of the meter scale. For example, the output of the photocell may be .002 milliampere. This would exceed the maximum reading on the scale of a 0-to-.001-milliampere meter. In such a case, a resistance can be connected in series with the photocell and the meter to reduce the current to a value which will be indicated by the meter. This can be accomplished with ordinary ½-watt radio resistors. The amount of resistance required will probably be between 100 and 500 ohms. Access to two 100-ohm resistors and one 270-ohm resistor will make it possible for you to place either 100, 200, 270, 370, or 470 ohms in the circuit by using one or more.

Chapter Fifteen

Rusting and Corrosion
Are Electrochemical Processes

Most metals have a tendency to react chemically with water, oxygen, carbon dioxide, and other substances normally found in the atmosphere. This process is called corrosion. It weakens and destroys metal structures and metal objects. One form of corrosion, called rusting, which occurs in iron and steel, causes loss and damage amounting to hundreds of millions of dollars per year.

Most efforts to prevent rust and corrosion of steel and iron involve coating the metal with a protective paint or with another metal. The common metals used to protect steel and iron are zinc, tin, cadmium, chromium, copper, lead, and nickel. Both electroplating and hot-dipping methods of coating are employed. Hot dipping consists of immersing clean steel or iron in a molten bath of the protective metal. Galvanized iron is sheet steel which has been coated thinly with zinc either by hot dipping or by electroplating.

A widely used protective coating is tin plating. A heavy coat of tin is generally applied to steel by hot dipping. Electroplating methods are used to apply thin coats. The so-called "tin" cans and containers which are a part of our living today are actually made of sheet steel coated with a very thin layer of tin. Tin costs more than other common metals and there is a limited supply. Known deposits of tin ores in the United States are either too small or too low-grade to make a significant contribution to the national supply. Tin imported into this country from Sumatra via the Suez Canal and the Mediterranean cost as much as $1.82 per pound in 1953. During the last decade the price of tin has more than doubled in price and is several times the cost of steel, copper, or aluminum.

The coating of tin on a "tin" can is purposely very thin because of the comparatively high cost of the metal. The can industry used about 45 per cent less tin per container in 1950 than in 1941. Although the canning industry still uses an enormous amount of steel, aluminum is being used increasingly for soft drinks and other beverages.

The steel used in making tin cans is principally iron. It contains also carbon and some impurities but can be considered as iron in its ordinary chemical action. For the remainder of this discussion, we will use the term "iron" instead of "sheet steel."

If an empty tin can is thrown away where it will be on the ground and exposed to the weather for several weeks, it will undergo considerable chemical and physical change. The coating of tin is not thick enough to protect the underlying iron for long and prevent it from becoming coated with the reddish brown substance which we know as rust. Given sufficient time, the iron will change completely into rust. Close examination and any tests which you may care to make will show that there is no similarity between the original iron and the resultant rust. The iron has undergone chemical change. The rusting of iron and steel is a slow oxidation of these metals which can eventually destroy them. Iron rust consists of oxides of iron more or less hydrated.

The rusting of iron is an ELECTROCHEMICAL action in which oxygen dissolved in water plays an essential part. Metals do not react at ordinary temperatures with the atmospheric gases except in the presence of water either in vapor or liquid form. Boiling water will drive out air dissolved in the water. Let us investigate what happens when a piece of clean, polished iron is placed in water and boiled until all air is driven out of the water. If the container is sealed immediately so that the atmosphere cannot reach the water, the iron WILL NOT RUST for a long time, because there is no oxygen in the water and none readily available. If the water is allowed to come into contact with the atmosphere long enough to reabsorb some oxygen, in a few hours the iron will show signs of rusting.

THE ELECTROCHEMICAL PROCESS OF RUSTING

There is more than one theory as to what actually happens in detail when iron or steel rusts. There is much evidence that an electrochemical action takes place on the surface of the metal. The most popular explanation is that multitudes of tiny voltaic cells are formed on the surface of the metal. The surface of ordinary iron and steel contains many specks of carbon and metallic impurities. If the surface becomes damp or wet and this water is exposed to air, it will contain dissolved carbon dioxide, oxygen, oxides of nitrogen, and other impurities which will make the water a weak electrolyte, able to conduct an electric current to some extent. The iron, the specks of impurities in the surface of the iron, and the conducting water solution of gases provide all the essentials of tiny voltaic cells. The iron has the tendency to send a few ferrous ions into the solution and to displace hydrogen. Wherever hydrogen ions are produced in this manner, hydroxyl ions must also be liberated. The ferrous ions will be changed to ferric ions and oxidized by the oxygen dissolved in the water to form ferric oxide (Fe_2O_3) with more or less water in its molecules—in other words, rust.

This theory of the electrochemical character of rusting also explains that it is not necessary for impurities to be present on the surface of the iron in order for rusting to start. Various spots on a single piece of iron may have slightly different activities and tendencies to send ferrous ions into the solution. One part of the metal may become more positive and another more negative than another. This may be due to stresses and strains set up in fabricating and cooling the iron.

The following experiments provide reasonable evidence that the electrochemical actions described above occur in the rusting of iron.

The exceedingly minute quantities of hydrogen evolved during the slow rusting of iron would be very difficult to detect. This problem can be solved easily in an indirect manner. Where hydrogen is thus evolved, hydroxyl ions also must be liberated. The presence of hydroxyl ions is easily revealed by a phenolphthalein solution. This indicator turns from colorless to red when brought into contact with hydroxyl ions. Therefore in our experiment we will look for hydroxyl ions, knowing that if they are present hydrogen is being evolved. We can employ a solution of potassium ferricyanide to detect iron ions. Ferricyanide ions in a solution of potassium ferricyanide form an insoluble blue compound when they meet with iron ions.

Since motion of the solutions used in the experiments would mix the red and blue indications, so that the results would be worthless, a jelly is used.

EXPERIMENT. Dissolve 1 gram of agar-agar (a Japanese sea plant obtainable at many drugstores) in 100 cubic centimeters of boiling water in a double boiler. When the agar-agar has dissolved, add a few drops of phenolphthalein and potassium cyanide solutions. The potassium cyanide solution must be freshly prepared by dissolving a few small crystals in 2 or 3 tablespoonfuls of water. When left standing, this solution undergoes changes which make it useless for the experiments. It MUST be freshly prepared.

Pour enough of the hot jelly containing the phenolphthalein and potassium ferricyanide solutions into a sauce dish to cover the bottom to a depth of about ¼ inch. Allow the jelly to cool and harden. Thoroughly wash two bright iron nails in order to remove all traces of any alkali or acid used to "pickle" the nails at the nail factory. Wipe both nails dry and place them on the hardened agar-agar. Melt the jelly remaining in the double boiler by heating it. Pour the softened jelly over the nails in the dish and allow it to harden undisturbed.

In the course of two or three hours, corrosion and rusting of the nails will be made evident by discoloration of the jelly. Red and blue areas indicating the presence of hydroxyl ions and iron ions will be plainly noticeable. The iron ions seem to have a tendency to go forth from the head and point of each nail. This is probably due to the fact that the iron has been subjected to more strain and stress at these points during the process of heading and pointing.

EXPERIMENTS WHICH DEMONSTRATE THAT THE RUSTING OF IRON IS AN ELECTROCHEMICAL ACTION

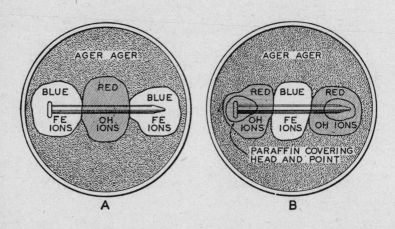

EXPERIMENT.   Repeat the last experiment but, before the nails are embedded in the jelly, cover their heads and points with hot paraffin wax so that these portions are protected from contact with the jelly. In the course of two or three hours, discoloration of the jelly will indicate that hydroxyl ions (indicated by red) are present near the ends of the nails instead of iron ions (indicated by blue) as in the first experiment.

The Use of Electrolysis to Prevent Rust and Corrosion

The method of preventing the rusting and corrosion of iron and steel most commonly employed is to protect the surface with a coating of paint, lacquer, tin, zinc, etc. This method protects merely by mechanically preventing access of moisture and air to the metal surface.

Another method of providing resistance to corrosion and rusting utilizes the electrochemical nature of the process. This method is often used to protect tanks, boilers, pipelines, and other iron and steel objects where the inside surface is not readily accessible. For example, in the case of a steel tank or boiler, stainless steel bars or magnesium bars are placed inside the boiler or tank. The bars are connected to the tank or boiler and become positive in respect to it. A small electric current then flows from the bars to the tank or boiler. The more active metal, that is, the stainless steel or the magnesium, then corrodes fairly rapidly. But the steel or iron in the tank or boiler is protected because it is an anode and anodes do not corrode. Small magnesium bars to protect household hot-water tanks by this method are available at plumbing shops and hardware stores.

Chapter Sixteen

Electrochemical Telegraphy

In the nineteenth century, when many inventors were endeavoring to produce a practical electric telegraph, attempts were made to perfect electrochemical telegraphs. Some of these were successful but were not so practical as the electromagnetic telegraph invented by Samuel Morse and so they were abandoned.

Usually the plan was this: An electric current was sent out over a wire and was broken up into dots and dashes which corresponded to the code letters of a telegraph alphabet. At the receiving station the current was sent through a strip of chemically prepared moist paper. Wherever the current passed through the paper, it discolored it. A dot would produce a small spot on the paper; a dash would produce a line. Thus it was easy to read the message. You will understand the principle of the electrochemical telegraph systems better after you have performed the next experiment.

Electrochemical Writing

EXPERIMENT. Dissolve 1 teaspoonful of sodium iodide or potassium iodide in 4 ounces of water. Set the solution aside temporarily. Then stir a piece of ordinary laundry starch about as large as a pea in 3 ounces of cold water. Heat this gently until it comes to a boil and then allow it to cool. When it is cool, add the sodium iodide or potassium iodide solution and stir the mixture well.

Brush both sides of a clean sheet of mimeograph paper with the starch-iodide mixture and spread the paper out smoothly on the bottom of a clean aluminum baking pan. The pan should be connected to the negative terminal of a battery of four or five No. 6 dry cells in series. Connect a 5-inch length of $\frac{1}{16}$-inch copper or brass rod to the positive terminal of the battery and use it as a stylus to write or draw on the paper.

Black lines will appear wherever the stylus is drawn

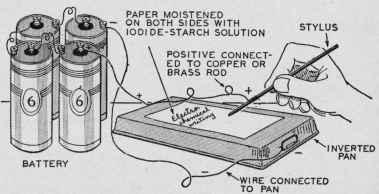

ELECTROCHEMICAL WRITING

PAPER MOISTENED ON BOTH SIDES WITH IODIDE-STARCH SOLUTION

STYLUS

POSITIVE CONNECTED TO COPPER OR BRASS ROD

Electro chemical writing

INVERTED PAN

BATTERY

WIRE CONNECTED TO PAN

across the surface of the paper. The explanation is simple. The passage of electric current through the paper frees iodine ions in the solution from their electric charge and they become iodine atoms ready to react with any suitable atoms. They react with starch to produce the blue-black color which is typical of the reaction between iodine and starch. The experiment will succeed equally well if a 10-volt bell-ringing or toy transformer is used in place of dry cells.

Red, White, and Blue

The fact that electrochemical action can bring about changes in a solution which result in the formation of colors is the basis of the next experiment.

EXPERIMENT. Add a few drops of alcoholic phenolphthalein solution to some of the starch iodide solution prepared for the last experiment. Pour this liquid into a glass "U" tube. (See illustration.) Push a small wad of absorbent cotton large enough to block off the horizontal portion of the tube to the bottom of each limb of the tube. Place a clean carbon rod from an old size D flashlight cell in each limb of the "U" tube as an electrode. Each carbon rod should have a short length of wire soldered to the brass cap on the upper end. Connect one carbon electrode to the positive terminal of a battery of three dry cells connected in series, and the other carbon electrode to the negative terminal.

At first the liquid in the tube will remain colorless, but after the electric current has flowed through it for a short time the solution surrounding the negative carbon will

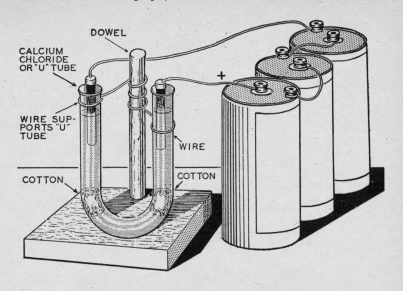

CALCIUM CHLORIDE OR "U" TUBE

DOWEL

WIRE SUPPORTS "U" TUBE

+

WIRE

COTTON

COTTON

THE "RED, WHITE, AND BLUE" EXPERIMENT

turn red, while the solution surrounding the positive carbon will turn blue. The solution between the two cotton plugs will remain colorless.

Explanation.   There are ions of potassium and iodine in the solution. The iodine ions (negative) are attracted to the positive electrode. There they lose their electric charge and form ordinary iodine atoms which react with the starch to form a blue color. The potassium ions (positive) are attracted to the negative electrode, where they lose their electric charge and form potassium hydroxide. The phenolphthalein trurns red in the presence of the alkaline potassium hydroxide. The cotton plugs prevent the red and blue portions of the solution from diffusing and mixing together.

Chemical Polarity Indicator

When the polarity indicator is connected to a source of direct current, it will show which wire is positive and which is negative. A reddish color will form about the carbon rod connected to the negative terminal.

EXPERIMENT. The indicator is made by passing two small flashlight cell carbons through tight-fitting holes in the cork for a small, wide-mouthed bottle. The carbon electrodes dip into a solution of sodium chloride contained in the bottle. Before putting the cork into the bottle, add eight or ten drops of phenolphthalein solution to the salt solution. Connect the polarity indicator to a 6-volt storage battery or to a battery of two or three dry cells connected in series. In a few seconds the solution around the carbon electrode connected to the negative battery terminal turns red. The red color may be eliminated by shaking the bottle.

POLARITY INDICATOR

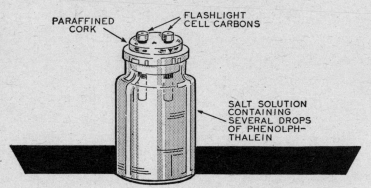

PARAFFINED CORK

FLASHLIGHT CELL CARBONS

SALT SOLUTION CONTAINING SEVERAL DROPS OF PHENOLPH-THALEIN

* Index

NaOH = lye